MW01712352

The Peasant and the Pen

aus
american
university
studies

Series XXIV
American Literature

Vol. 75

PETER LANG
New York • Washington, D.C./Baltimore • Bern
Frankfurt am Main • Berlin • Brussels • Vienna • Oxford

George Guida

The Peasant and the Pen

Men, Enterprise, and the Recovery of Culture in Italian American Narrative

PETER LANG
New York • Washington, D.C./Baltimore • Bern
Frankfurt am Main • Berlin • Brussels • Vienna • Oxford

Library of Congress Cataloging-in-Publication Data

Guida, George.
The peasant and the pen: men, enterprise, and the recovery
of culture in Italian American narrative / George Guida.
p. cm. — (American university studies.
Series XXIV, American literature; vol. 75)
Includes bibliographical references and index.
1. American literature—Italian American authors—
History and criticism. 2. Italian Americans—Biography—
History and criticism. 3. Italian Americans in literature.
4. Men in literature. I. Title. II. Series.
PS153.I8 G85 810.9'851—dc21 2002154661
ISBN 0-8204-6730-8
ISSN 0895-0512

Bibliographic information published by **Die Deutsche Bibliothek**.
Die Deutsche Bibliothek lists this publication in the "Deutsche
Nationalbibliografie"; detailed bibliographic data is available
on the Internet at http://dnb.ddb.de/.

The paper in this book meets the guidelines for permanence and durability
of the Committee on Production Guidelines for Book Longevity
of the Council of Library Resources.

275 Seventh Avenue, 28th Floor, New York, NY 10001
www.peterlangusa.com

Printed in Germany

To my parents,
my sisters,
and my wife,
who are always with me

Contents

PREFACE

This book is intended for students and scholars new to the study of Italian American literature and culture. When I imagine its audience, I imagine students in my Italian American and immigration studies courses at the State University of New York at Stony Brook; or I imagine my colleagues at New York City College of Technology who have often asked me, "So what's Italian American literature?" With this audience in mind, I have tried to write a book that assumes limited knowledge of both the texts it examines and of Italian American history.

I hope that seasoned scholars in the field will bear with explanations of familiar terms and ideas, and look instead to some of the issues my analyses raise and some of the texts I analyze. I believe these texts provide important insights into Italian American male identity, Italian American culture, and Italian American narrative.

George Guida
Brooklyn, New York

ACKNOWLEDGMENTS

Thanks to Bob Viscusi and Neil Tolchin, for introducing me to Italian American literature as such. Thanks to Anthony Valerio, Morris Dickstein, Bill Kelly, Fred Gardaphè, Phil Cannistraro, Maria Mazziotti Gillan, James DeJongh and Joan Richardson, for guiding and encouraging me. Thanks to Francesco Sorrentino, Ambrose Franceschini, Damian Catani, Giuseppe Amendola, and David Castronuovo, for helping me learn Italian under duress. Thanks to Vittoria Repetto, Nancy Caronia, Peter Carravetta, Adele Regina LaBarre, Stephen Cooper, Ed Hack, and Nancy Berke, for sharing our work. Thanks to Chris Cesare and James Berger, for being constant friends. And thanks, of course, to my Italian American family and my honorary Italian American wife, Pam Ouellette, for tolerating a writer in the house.

I would also like to thank the following for their permission to reprint from the following works:

Stephen Cooper and David Fine, eds. *John Fante: A Critical Gathering.* Copyright 1999. Reprinted by permission of Fairleigh Dickinson University Press. All rights reserved.

John Fante. *Ask the Dust.* Copyright 1991. Reprinted by permission of HaperCollins Publishers, Inc. All rights reserved.

John Fante. *The Wine of Youth: Selected Stories.* Copyright 1991. Reprinted by permission of HarperCollins Publishers. All rights reserved.

John Fante. *Wait Until Spring, Bandini.* Copyright, 1989. Reprinted by permission of HarperCollins Publishers. All rights reserved.

George Guida. "Giovanni Verga and the Roots of Italian America."
This article was first published in *Italian Americana* 21.2 (Summer 2003), published at University of Rhode Island—Providence, 80 Washington Street, Providence, Rhode Island 02903. It is reprinted by permission of the journal. All rights reserved.

George Guida. "Novel *Paesans:* The Reconstruction of Italian-American Male Identity in Anthony Valerio's *Conversation with Johnny* and Robert Viscusi's *Astoria,*" *MELUS* 26.2 (Summer 2001): 95–108. Reprinted by permission of the journal.

Ed Hack. unpublished paper on Anthony Valerio. Copyright 1998. Reprinted by permission of the author.

Anthony Valerio. *Conversation with Johnny.* Copyright Anthony Valerio, Guernica Editions 1997. Reprinted by permission of Guernica Editions.

Anthony Valerio. Interview with George Guida. *Italian Matters.* Public Access Television, New York, 7 Feb. 1995. Quoted by permission of the interviewee.

Anthony Valerio. Interview with Leonard Lopate. *New York and Company.* Natl. Public Radio. WNYC, New York. 7 August 1997. Quoted by permission of the interviewee.

Anthony Valerio. Personal interview. 5 December 1996. Quoted by permission of the interviewee.

Anthony Valerio. "The Skyjacker," *The Paris Review* 73 (Winter 1977): 80–86. Reprinted by permission of the *The Paris Review.*

Anthony Valerio. *Valentino and the Great Italians, According to Anthony Valerio.* Copyright Anthony Valerio, Guernica Editions 1994. Reprinted by permission of the Guernica Editions.

Introduction

A Search for Place: Tracing the Sources of Italian American Identity and Italian American Narrative

"*Tutt'a posto,*" my great-grandfather Pietro Patelli would say, meaning "everything in place." For my great-grandfather, "*tutt'a posto*" meant more particularly that the daily affairs of his American construction company were settled. Satisfied that his men had secured the company's Lower East Side subway site for the night, he could settle into the lacquered cherry wood throne of his backyard grape arbor and puff his pipe through the early Brooklyn evening.

When a few years back I went to live and study Italian culture at a Tuscan university hundreds of miles and a hundred years removed from my great-grandfather's *paese,* his hometown in Campania—the 5,346,828 square-mile region of Italy, stretching from the Tyrrhenian Sea east to the spine of the Appenine mountain range, and from the Roman region of Lazio south to the southernmost mainland region of Calabria—I discovered that for most Italians it remains important to have *tutt'a posto.*

"*Tutt'a posto?*" questioned Signor Pinciani, the university's *Direttore* of student housing, pointing to my room.

"*Tutt'a posto?*" Fabio, a law student from Calabria, inquired, pointing to me.

"*Sì,*" I answered them both, believing that, after wandering through two medieval cities, toting five leaden bags and a guitar case, enough of my American life to sustain me for the year abroad, having scared up enough Italian to request a room key, I had managed finally to find my assigned dormitory and lay my burden on the room's cold tile floor just in time to collapse on my steel-frame cot for a three-hour nap, that everything was now indeed in its place.

But I was deluded, a self-satisfied American dreaming the transition to a new language and culture would be simple. Quickly, I learned that everything was not even close to what most Italians I know are comfortable calling in place. To achieve true equilibrium, I had first to find a proper *way* for everything I did, a proper place for everything I owned: clothes *neatly* folded and stowed, bed sheets tucked *tightly* under the mattress, classes *carefully* scheduled, language mastered, diet controlled, courtesies politely dispensed, mind, body, and spirit contented.

I have since discovered that, contrary to two possible and frequent stereotypes of Italians as brutes and profligates, the desire for place, for order, remains an Italian obsession—and from an historical perspective, an understandable one. For centuries, the peoples of the Italian peninsula, especially those of Southern Italy, have needed to preserve property, dignity, and often their very lives from a ceaseless procession of occupying forces and exploitative governments. In the Italy of my sojourn, the obsession for order manifested itself in Signor Pinciani's insistence on "*la pulizia della camera,*" the cleanliness and order of each and every dorm room; or in a twenty year-old (male) university student's mopping his floor twice a week; or in another student's determination, at the university dining hall, to have me eat the *primo piatto primo* and the *secondo secondo.* In America, it appears in the careful arrangement of Capodimonte figurines in my mother's china cabinet, her well-laid plans for my sisters'catering hall weddings and future residence not too many miles away from home; in the painstakingly placed ceramic lions and donkeys of Bensonhurst's front yards; and, I am surprised to discover, in my own desire to set Italian American narrative *tutt'a posto.*

My great-grandfather read the Italian American newspaper *Il Progresso Italo-Americano* every day, but he never read an Italian American book, a book about Italian American experience. Still, my great-grandfather's spirit, his zeal for order, lives on in this book about Italian American books. In his spirit this book attempts to identify and describe characteristic relationships between Italian American narrative, Italian American men, and their heritage; between Italian American narrative, Italian culture, and American culture. I call the sum of these relationships *impresa/ripresa.* While *impresa/ripresa* does not consist of a single narrative pattern or model that may be derived or made to fit *all* Italian American narrative texts, it does identify a pair of recurring tendencies in many of these texts: enterprise and recovery.

Impresa and *ripresa*, enterprise and recovery, work in tandem to limn the salient feature of all serious literary narrative: a narrator's or character's identity, his or her self. The narrative self (narrator/protagonist) and the self's life story (plot) are products of the author's awareness of the self's particular culture(s) (Eakin xxi), and his or her ability to portray the self's cultural and linguistic acts of enterprise and recovery in terms intelligible to the narrative audience(s).

In Italian American narratives, authors manipulate narrative language and form to create selves identifying at once with Anglo American culture (and an Anglo American audience) and (a regional) Italian culture (and Italian and Italian American audiences). *Impresa/ripresa* is simply the sum of linguistic, formal and thematic ways that authors of Italian American narrative construct these complex selves. *Impresa* is the process by which these authors tell stories that reinforce the American myth of the self-made man, manifest in Benjamin Franklin's *Autobiography* and Horatio Alger's "luck and pluck" boy books. In contrast, *Ripresa* is the process by which these same authors criticize American life (and the individual's pursuit of its material rewards), by comparing it to an idealized life—often a life of the mind—in Europe or more specifically Italy or even more specifically *Mezzogiorno* communities similar to those that nineteenth-century Italian Sicilian author Giovanni Verga recreates in his short stories. The values (family, honor and respect) of these communities are clearly less individualistic than the values of nineteenth- and twentieth-century America. *Ripresa* is thus a version of pastoral in which Italian American authors reconstitute Old World culture and society as spiritual, intellectual, and sentimental ballast for the ship of self they construct to master their worldly sea of striving and success in America.

*Impresa/*Ripresa applies especially to those Italian Americans most subject, by virtue of their public lives, to popular scrutiny and discussion across the twentieth century: Italian American men. In America, as in Italian American narrative, Italian American men have struggled with the dilemma of shrouded, complex identities in a society that has historically treated the Mediterranean and other non-Nordic male with suspicion. Italian American male authors have written, not surprisingly, accounts of Italian American male identity that incorporate problems and triumphs peculiar to the Italian American male psyche.

In two early twentieth-century autobiographies, "The Biography of a Bootblack" and *Personal Reminiscences of a Naturalized American*, Rocco Corresca and Francesco Ventresca, both Italian immigrants, tell tales of an American *impresa* inflected by the *ripresa* of Italian (European) life and honor. Corresca's is a story of thrift, industry, and good fortune, worthy of Franklin and Alger, but written in the voice of a man mediating between an American audience eager to have their belief in the possibility of rising reinforced and an Italian audience eager to make their fortunes in America, but ignorant and perhaps suspicious of American society. Ventresca's story recounts the enterprise of establishing himself as a successful and influential American educator and government official, while it expresses an enduring feeling of connection to his native Italy and the rest of European society, culture, and language.

In his Arturo Bandini tetralogy, John Fante, an Italian American author writing of life in post-World War I Colorado and Depression-Era California, records the *impresa*, the upward literary and romantic struggles, of his protagonist, while demonstrating his sense of Italian ethnic identity, his desire to recapture a pre-Anglo America and explore a pan-ethnic sense of difference from the Anglo American mainstream. And in the contemporary novel, *Valentino and the Great Italians*, and *Lefty and the Button Men*, Anthony Valerio, a native of Bensonhurst, Brooklyn—America's largest Little Italy—and a pioneer post-modern Italian American writer, redefines his male characters' sense of masculinity and Americanness, by linking their ambitions and experiences in contemporary society with those of illustrious Italians and Italian Americans of the past.

That past is a modern past radiating from Italian American culture's *posto* of origin, the nineteenth-century *Mezzogiorno,* a place I foolishly tried to locate in contemporary Tuscany.

Chapter 1

THE CULTURE THAT TIME FORGOT: NINETEENTH-CENTURY *MEZZOGIORNO* SOCIETY AND THE STORIES OF GIOVANNI VERGA

A medieval via, narrow, dark, runs through the heart of Prata del Principato Ultra, a town in Campania, thirty miles inland from Naples, from which both my paternal great-grandfather and maternal grandfather emigrated to New York. The via begins in the town's lone *piazza*, where, under the midday sun of the *Mezzogiorno*—the land named for the midday sun—men lounged on benches, played *briscola*, sipped *espressi*, eyeballed me as I walked from a lonely bus stop to the flower shop called "Preziosi," a family name. Down the via barely wide enough for a Fiat, I walked past one–story stone hovels and vistas of backyard gardens and vaguely green hills beyond; past women wearing black, sitting in windows; past blind alleys leading to dead public courtyards. All of this, the source.

The *Mezzogiorno* of Italy is truly "the land that time forgot" (Gambino, *Blood* 230): both now, for me, a fellow on spring break from a Northern Italian university, and a century ago, for my great-grandfather, an apprentice with no prospect of becoming *maestro* in his own *paese*. The *Mezzogiorno*: a land comprised of eight Southern regions—The Abruzzi, Campania, Molise, Apulia, Basilicata (formerly Lucania), Calabria, Sicily, and Sardinia—then, as now, the most underdeveloped and archaic area of Italy. Even after 1861, the year in which most of Italy was unified and became, nominally, a liberal nation-state, peasants of the *Mezzogiorno* continued to live according to centuries-old economic and social customs. A full generation after the Risorgimento, the unification of Italy, less than ten percent of the total population of Italy was eligible to vote; and Italian law of the period effectively barred entry into government to all but wealthy landlords (Mack Smith 236).

From 1880 to 1910, the Italian government commissioned two wide-ranging (although flawed) studies of conditions in the *Mezzogiorno*: The Jacini Investigation (1878–1885) and the Faini Investigation (1907–1910). Both were essentially fact-finding missions whose purposes were to determine the causes and nature of *La Miseria*—the dire condition of Southern peasants, brought on by a complex of extreme economic and social problems (Mangione and

Morreale 45)—and to suggest remedies. Unfortunately, these missions did little to alleviate the peasants' economic and social woes, which persist to a lesser degree in the lives of contemporary *Meridionali* (residents of the *Mezzogiorno*) (Manoukian 13–34).

The tragedy of *La Miseria* reveals itself in the work of Sicilian author Giovanni Verga. Although he was not himself a peasant, Verga sought to interpret the world of the peasants in their own terms. Born in 1840, in Catania, Sicily, to an aristocratic family, Verga at age twenty-five published his first novel and moved to Florence, and then, eight years later, to Milan. During the 1870s, he published autobiographical novels of upper-class romantic intrigue, all of which reflect the influence of French realism, but none of which stands as a literary achievement of any great merit.

In the mid 1870s, Verga turned his attention to the subject of his later masterpieces, the way of life of southern Italian, particularly Sicilian, peasants. That way of life inspired two great novels, *I Malavoglia* (1881) and *Maestro Don Gesualdo* (1889); and two superb collections of short stories, *Vita dei Campi* (1880) and *Novelle Rusticane* (1883) (the collections originally translated into English by D. H. Lawrence).

Verga's Sicilians live the lives of most late nineteenth-century *contadini,* the peasants of the *Mezzogiorno*. Their condition, often their survival, depended upon the year's harvest. And as it often has for the world's peasants, poverty set the tone of their lives. It fueled passions and unexpected violence that disrupted a seemingly idyllic existence (Cecchetti, "Introduction" xii). As has also often been the case for peasants, the social lives of Southern Italian peasants were governed by a rigid moral code. Simply to maintain their humble place in society, these beleaguered people had constantly to check their desires. One affront to the honor of woman or family, one protest to his landlord, could spell the peasant's end. This condition is the lens through which Verga's Sicilian tales project peasant life.

The types of people who inhabit Verga's tales—day laborers, small land owners, shepherds, and other economically marginal figures—accounted for up to two-thirds of the population of many Sicilian towns (Gabaccia 6). Verga's peasants are proud people accustomed to misery, seeking whatever joy they can find in their difficult lives. The author captures the details and values of their traditional world in a dignified rendition of their own language and thought patterns—a technique later employed by several important Italian American novelists, notably Pietro di Donato.

Verga's tales portray both the economic predicament of Southern peasants and their resulting sense of impotence to alter their situation: a situation that fosters a typically Sicilian, tragic view of life (Toschi 14). Since the peasant life that Verga depicts has with rare exception vanished from the *Mezzogiorno*, his literary recreation is as near an experience of actual nineteenth-century peasant existence, and of the future migrants' consciousness, as we have.

In general, Verga's stories convey a strong sense of *campanilismo*—the peasants' limitation and attachment to their town and its environs—and their suspicion of outsiders. They convey also, at every turn, the effects of poverty. Verga's third-person narrators speak as fellow villagers, as if they are reminding readers, not necessarily informing them, of the village personae and local places they describe. Yet, they speak with knowledge beyond the limits of the villager's consciousness. This balance between identification and distance from subject lends Verga's voice a journalistic objectivity that renders the tragedy of his tales even more shocking and powerful. Witness the opening lines of a tale upon which Leoncavallo based a classic opera, *"Cavalleria Rusticana"* (1880): "When Turiddu Macca, Nunzia's son, came back from the service, he used to strut in the square on Sundays in his *bersagliere* uniform with the red cap that looked like the one worn by the fortuneteller who sets up a bench with a cage of canaries" (10). For the townspeople, with whom the narrator shares certain knowledge (of a particular kind of fortuneteller, for instance), Turiddu, an impoverished former soldier, is both an object of admiration and resentment; a familiar and a man in uniform representing an indifferent, suspicious government. The mixed feelings that he inspires within the community ultimately seal his doom.

Like Turiddu, the protagonists of Verga's tales contend with the various hardships that forced so many peasants to emigrate. All three characters in "Black Bread" (1882)—Santo, Lucia (Santo's sister), and Nena (Santo's wife)—work like dogs in order to eat. Lucia resents their lot, even as she accepts it; and at various points, she expresses this sort of class resentment, which was common among *contadini* of the day (Mangione and Morreale 48–53). From her point of view, we understand the interplay of economic and social life. "That crook of a field watchman had done himself a favor by marrying off his daughter [Nena] without a dowry, and now it was up to Santo to support her. Since Nena had been with him, Santo saw that he didn't have enough bread for both of them and they would have to snatch it by the sweat of their brow from the land…" (Verga 172). For her part, Lucia realizes too late that the only way to have saved her dying mother would have been to accede to the unwanted romantic advances and dowry of an older *galantuomo* (or gentleman), a member of the landowning upper class. In this world, the wish for marriage, like the wish for salvation, comes at a heavy price.

As common in the *Mezzogiorno* as class conflict and repressed desire was illness: illness arising from the peasants' very sustenance, the land. In the wake of the Risorgimento, a new crop of landlords set about clearing large tracts of Southern forests, in attempts to maximize agricultural profits. Deforestation soon led to soil erosion, which turned areas of formerly hospitable valleys into marshes, breeding grounds for malaria-carrying insects (Nelli 20). Peasants often walked miles each day through these marshes, from their hill towns to the fields they worked. Many contracted malaria.

Verga allows us to feel the ravages of the disease as the peasants felt them, in his 1881 tale "Malaria". The narrator of the tale uses malaria as a vivid metaphor for the peasants' desperate condition. "Malaria," he remarks, "gets into your bones with the bread you eat" (Verga 118). He goes on to describe the effects of the disease from the peasant perspective. Malaria "snatches up the villagers in the deserted streets and nails them in front of the door of their houses plasterless from the sun, and they shake with fever under their overcoats and under all the bed blankets piled upon their shoulders" (118). Verga changes the tone of his narrative voice here from folkloric ("snatches up the villagers") and Christian ("nails them in front of the door") to documentary ("they shake with fever"). For him, malaria is a metaphorical and mythical plague, as well as a literal disease. It precipitates the peasants' flight from a homeland that is also ancient Egypt; as it is a cause of emigration rooted in socio-economic depredation akin to the worst systems of feudalism and slavery.[1] Day in and day out, the peasants endure malaria at work and play, escaping it only when they leave, because as "Wife-killer" (a character whose several wives all die of the disease) reasons, "for those people there just isn't malaria!" (127). Unless and until, like many real *contadini* of the period, Verga's peasants overcome their fatalism and emigrate, they simply assume the risks and accept the frequently fatal consequences as a fact of life in the *Mezzogiorno*.

Prefiguring Tomasi di Lampedusa's *Il Gattopardo*, Verga's tale "Freedom" recounts yet another peasant hardship, disappointment with the Risorgimento. The story begins, "They hung the tricolor kerchief [the flag of united Italy] from the campanile, sounded the alarm with the bells, and began to shout in the square: 'Hail to freedom!'" (206). It ends, "The charcoal man, while they were handcuffing him again, stammered: 'Where are you taking me? To jail? Why? I didn't even get a foot of land. And they had said there was freedom!...'" (216). The freedom Garibaldi's liberators promised evolves into a new form of imprisonment of the peasants, their jailers now the civil authorities that the *Garibaldini* helped to establish.

From the 1860s through the 1880s, disastrous agricultural practices, along with an onerous system of taxation, plunged the peasants even deeper into *La Miseria*. Corrupt landowners and ruthless overseers went unchecked by a distant government whose policies reflected its own susceptibility to corruption. As land grew less productive through mismanagement, taxes rose until they were the highest in Europe (Nelli 23), and inequitable. Cows, usually owned by wealthy landlords, were not taxable commodities; mules, usually owned by *contadini* (and used by Verga as symbols of peasant suffering and survival) were (Mangione and Morreale 63). The peasants, though no longer serfs, were now slaves to capital.

It may be difficult for us to imagine how the peasants of the Mezzogiorno survived the wrath of all the forces—social, natural, political, economic—arrayed against them, but, as Verga's tales also show, they do. In "Property" (1882), they survive through ceaseless work and *furberia* (cleverness, cunning) (Gambino, *Blood* 134). The protagonist of "Property," Mazzarò, embodies *furberia*. His name itself echoes both the Sicilian *massaro,* one given to "diligent application" of himself (Gabaccia 6), and the Italian *amazzare,* "to kill," suggesting all at once Mazzarò's all-consuming diligence, his social and spiritual suicide, and his symbolic killing off of masters. "He had gotten together all that property himself, with his hands and with his mind, by not sleeping at night, by catching fever from anxiety or from malaria, by toiling from morning till night, and going around in the sun and in the rain, by wearing out his boots and his mules..." (Verga 143–44). Mazzarò has not achieved the ends of property according to peasant values—the preservation of family and folkways—but he has mastered the means.

Although he has "no children, nor grandchildren, nor other relatives" (144) and no peace of mind, Mazzarò understands full well that "[p]roperty doesn't belong to those who have it, but to those who know how to get it'" (144). He understands too what the proprietor must do to maintain property.

"After he had gotten his property, he certainly didn't send word that he was coming to supervise the harvest or the vintage, and when and how, but turned up unexpectedly, on foot or on a mule, without watchmen, with a piece of bread in his pocket; and he slept near his sheaves, his eyes open, and his shotgun between his legs" (144–45). Mazzarò overcomes economic oppression only in this way, through a relentless effort that deprives him of familial, spiritual, even physical comfort. "So, when they told him that the time had come to leave his property and think of his soul, he staggered out into the courtyard like a madman" (147). The peasant is, and in reality frequently was, forced to choose between his livelihood on one hand, and his family and traditional values on the other.

In other tales Verga portrays, with both sympathy and scorn, the values and folkways that sustain peasants and, later, emigrants from the *Mezzogiorno.* In *"Cavalleria Rusticana,"* a young man, Turiddu, dies in the name of honor, at the hands of his true love's husband, Alfio. Forbidden to marry the beautiful Santa for lack of money, Turiddu becomes her lover. Alfio finds out and must defend his honor. The Southern Italian code of honor compelled the offended to respond quickly and decisively to whatever person had sullied his or his family's character. Adherents to this code, the *contadini*, held marriage as the fullest expression of family integrity and any challenge to an established marriage as the ultimate offense (Alba 33). A husband's honor, and his family's honor, depended upon his wife's (and his other female relatives') loyalty and shame (Rando 24). Anything less than restoration of honor would endanger the peasant's own economic and social status and that of his family, since family honor, its interplay with social status and property, formed the basis of useful social ties (Gabaccia IV, 9, 220). Turiddu recognizes Alfio's masculine obligation to defend his family's honor and agrees to a dual in which Alfio kills him. Triumphant, Alfio declares, "'That's for making a cuckold of me in my own house'" (18). Dying, Turiddu is tragic and grotesque. "For a while Turiddu staggered here and there among the cactuses and then fell like a log. Blood gurgled up and foamed in his throat, and he couldn't even gasp: *Ah, mamma mia!" (18).* He begins the tale as a popinjay marching in uniform through the town square, an object of admiration as well as resentment; and ends up like dog in the dust, an object of scorn, dead young, in service of the *Mezzogiorno* code of honor.

As much as they lived by this code of honor, the Southern Italian peasants lived by a complex system of superstitions and religious beliefs. In "Rosso Malpelo" and "War Between Saints" (1880), Verga renders important aspects of Southern pagan superstition and saint-worship. Many Sicilians, peasant and otherwise, believed that redheads had evil dispositions (Cecchetti, *Giovanni* 65), a belief which determines the fate of the story's protagonist, Malpelo (literally, "evil hair"). Superstitions like this one were common among the peasants, products of age-old uncertainty and vulnerability. Over the centuries, the *contadini's* Biblical vicissitudes led them to speculate that warring saints and demons dictated their destinies (Gambino, *Blood* 213–14), that free will, if it existed at all, was a relatively weak force.

From the outset of his story, superstition binds Malpelo. "He was called Malpelo because he had red hair; and he had red hair because he was a mean and bad boy, who promised to turn into a first-rate scoundrel. So everybody at the red-sand quarry called him Malpelo, and even his mother, having always heard that name, had almost forgotten his real one" (Verga 65). Verga makes clear that, like superstition itself, Malpelo's hair and name are self-fulfilling prophecies. Onto the young boy, Verga projects peasant fatalism. His narrator speaks with the voice of superstitious peasants, in his condemnation of the unfortunate lad. "[H]e would go and huddle in a corner," the narrator reveals, "his basket between his legs, to nibble his piece of dark bread, as *animals like him do*" (emphasis added) (Verga 66). Here, Verga compares Malpelo to a beast, valued for what he can do and not for who he is. No one cares for Malpelo, because of his red hair (Selig 35), a trait upon which the peasant consciousness of the narrative seizes as a means of explaining the boy's otherwise inexplicable malignancy; and because no one cares for him, he is sent to work on a dangerous project in the same quarry that killed his father. No "man with a family wanted to take a chance, nor would he let his own flesh and blood run such a risk for all the gold in the world. But as for Malpelo, he didn't even have anyone who would want to take all the gold in the world for his hide, if it was really worth that much: so they thought of him" (85). Malpelo does not protest this or any other mistreatment. "'What for?'" he asks, resigned, "I'm Malpelo'" (73). In the absolute, article-less manner of the Italian language, "Malpelo" is adjective as noun, defining identity as well as quality. (To say, for example, "I am a Southerner," one would say, *"Sono meridionale,"* not *"Sono* un *meridionale."*)

If the peasants believed that supernatural forces controlled their destinies, then for them no force was greater than their patron saints. In the *Mezzogiorno*, the peasant called upon his patron saint to bless the land, and he believed the saint's benediction would have a material, often immediate, effect (De Rosa 5). His interaction with his saint, as with God and the Holy Family, was personal, familiar (Gambino, *Blood* 221). Verga plumbs the depth of this belief in "War Between Saints." The narrator of the story recounts the battle for processional rights through a small town, between the devotees of Saint Rocco and those of Saint Paschal. Depending upon where they reside, the peasants pray to one or the other, for rain and immunity to cholera. To supplicate according to custom—a custom that survives to this day in Italy and Little Italies throughout the world (Orsi, "Religious" 330)—they march icons of the saints through town in ritual procession.

> In fact, they did carry Saint Paschal in procession, to the east and to the west, and they held him high on the hill to bless the fields, one sultry, cloudy day in May—one of those days when the farmers tear their hair in front of their burnt fields, and the wheatears bend down just as if they were dying (Verga 103).

Nino, one of these afflicted farmers, who lives in the rival district of Saint Rocco, blames his rivals' saint for his problems. "'Damned Saint Paschal!' he shouts, "spitting in the air, running through the wheat field like a madman. 'You've ruined me, Saint Paschal, you thief! All you've left me is a sickle to cut my throat with!'" (103)

Later, Nino heaps abuse on his own patron, who, as he sees it, has done equally little to improve his condition. "'Ah, Saint Rocco, you thief!' Nino began to lament. 'I didn't expect this from you!...' Ah, Saint Rocco!' said he. "This is a dirtier trick than Saint Paschal played on us!'" (106). His reliance, anger, imprecation of his own saint reflect the nature of Southern *contadino* saint worship, which could often end in outright iconoclasm and deposition of the patron in favor of another (Salamone-Marino 172–74).

Verga presents this peasant approach to worship as both charming and senseless. In his stories, Saints mean much to peasants, but do not materially change their lives. At the close of "War Between Saints," the two main characters, Nino and Saridda, recovering together from cholera, continue to argue the relative power of their patron saints, neither of whom has done anything to alleviate either drought or illness.

> "And you? Do you think it was Saint Rocco who kept you alive?"

> "Why don't you stop it!" broke in Saridda. "Or we'll need another cholera to make peace!" (Verga 107)

In Saridda's imperative we hear Verga's. This ironic tone of Saridda's retort, however, while it satirizes the peasants' reliance on saints to deliver them, stops short of discounting saint worship entirely. The *feste* surrounding it was, after all, one of the joys of peasant life.

Certainly, peasant life could, in many ways, be joyous and beautiful, even though, on the whole, it was nothing to inspire nostalgia. Yet, a longing for peasant life in the *Mezzogiorno* marks a great deal of Italian American narrative. That longing is often nostalgia for *bell'Italia*, the beautiful land itself. I have heard Italians remark, *"C'e il mare, c'e il sole. Che cos'altro ci vuole?"* ("We have the sea and the sun. What else do we need?"). Verga's "Ieli" (1880) turns on this sentiment, a deep feeling for the land, not only as soil, but also as landscape, idealized site of innocence and simplicity.

Ieli, a poor shepherd boy, and Don Alfonso, the young son of a wealthy landowner, share days together in the pastures.

> Ah, the wonderful chases over the mown fields, manes in the wind! the beautiful days of April, when the wind piled up the green grass into waves and the mares neighed in the pastures! the beautiful summer afternoons, when the whitish countryside lay silent under the hazy sky, and the grasshoppers crackled among the clods, as if the stubble were catching fire! the beautiful winter sky through the naked branches of the almond tree that shivered in the north wind, and the path that sounded frozen under the horses' hoofs, and the skylarks that sang high up in the warmth, in the blue! the beautiful summer evenings that came up very slowly, like fog, the good smell of the hay in which you sank your elbows, and the melancholy humming of the evening insects, and those two notes of Ieli's pipe, always the same—ee-oo! Ee-oo! Ee-oo! (20)

The tone of reminiscence in this passage foreshadows the loss of innocence and simplicity of which Ieli's life becomes a symbol; an innocence and simplicity that Don Alfonso and, later, immigrants from Italy, convinced themselves they had had and lost; an imaginary, timeless life (Boelhower, *Immigrant* 103–08) that was in reality at least as miserable as it was innocent and simple.

Portions of "Ieli," like portions of many Italian American narratives, are pastoral reconstructions of life in the *Mezzogiorno*. Classical pastoral locates simplicity and innocence in the shepherd, presenting his life as (Christ-like) ideal. In the pastoral tale, the shepherd suffers and savors simple pleasures for the entire community (Marinelli 6). (The Italian title of the story has been translated as "Ieli the Shepherd.") Verga's pastoral, like those of Theocritus and the Italian American immigrant autobiographers, begins with an experienced adult looking back on an innocent childhood (10). As he grows older, Don Alfonso learns to read—which causes Ieli to look "at the book and at him suspiciously" (Verga 26). Don Alfonso then assumes his position in the rigid caste system (Covello 75) of the *Mezzogiorno*, the position of *galantuomo*. The *galantuomini* (gentlemen) were nobility, landowners associated, usually by blood, with baronial estates. They recognized each other's cultural and class superiority, and forced the lower social classes to do the same (97). After he has taken his rightful position and left Ieli behind in the fields, Don Alfonso has an affair with Mara, the woman who, in part because Don Alfonso ruins her reputation, agrees to marry Ieli.

Class distinction and Mara's attraction to Alfonso ultimately corrupt and destroy Ieli. Although his is mentally slow, Ieli slowly comes to recognize his wife's adultery with Alfonso and to feel a shame and anger about it that he cannot fully comprehend. During an argument, a shepherd boy tells Ieli what everyone else in the town already knows, that Don Alfonso "has taken your wife" (Verga 60). Labeled a "cuckold," the strongest of all insults in Southern Italy (Alba 34), even the gentle, unsuspecting Ieli must react. "Even when he thought of Don Alfonso, he couldn't believe that such a dirty trick was possible; he still could see him at Tebedi [the pasture lands], with his kind eyes and his smiling little mouth coming to bring sweets and white bread, so long ago—such a dirty trick! And since he hadn't seen him any more, for he was a poor shepherd who stayed in the country the whole year round, he always remembered him that way" (Verga 62). His wife's and Alfonso's corruption raise Ieli's consciousness of his limitation as peasant and his disgrace as cuckold, poisoning his contentment with the simple shepherd's life.

At a "picnic in the country at shearing time" (63), in the company of both Mara and Don Alfonso, Ieli is at first able to overcome incipient feelings of shame and anger, and enjoy the pastoral scene. From his point of view, so close to the natural world, we hear, "It was a beautiful, warm day in the golden fields with the flowering hedges and the long green rows of vines. The sheep were gamboling and bleating with pleasure at feeling themselves freed from all that wool, and in the kitchen the women were making a big fire to cook all the things that the owner had brought for dinner" (63). Still, amid the simple gaiety of the country outing—one of the peasants' few escapes from ceaseless labor and suffering (qtd. in Salamone-Marino 123)—Ieli is reminded of his class inferiority and his disgrace. "Meanwhile, the rich men who were waiting had gone into the shade under the carob trees, and were having someone play the tambourines and bagpipes, and those who wanted to, danced with the women of the farm" (Verga 63).

Even amid such delightful scenes, Don Alfonso's and Mara's corruption infects Ieli, and he finally succumbs. "Ieli, while he was shearing the sheep, felt something gnaw inside him, without knowing why, like a thorn, a driven nail, a pair of fine shears that worked around inside him bit by bit, worse than poison" (63). When, over Ieli's objections, Mara goes off to dance with Alfonso, Ieli slits Alfonso's throat with his shears, transforming from innocent to murderer and symbol of growing peasant discontent with the ongoing inequities of post-Risorgimento Italy.

To understand fully Verga's use of symbolism and other narrative elements, we need to recognize the prevalence, in nineteenth-century *Mezzogiorno* life, of the folktale, the timeless peasant narrative form and means of transmitting cultural and moral customs and lessons (Covello 266–68). Writing in 1960, Mario Pei recognized the lingering power of myth and legend in Southern Italian society. "Even today," wrote Pei, "the miraculous exploits of mythological and legendary heroes continue to be recounted by *cantastorie*, those often illiterate bards who wander from village to village" (Preface ix). In order to understand the Southern Italian peasant consciousness of cyclical time and attachment to elemental, pre-industrial life, as well as the influence of creeping capitalism upon that consciousness (Propp 17), we must account for the effect of this living tradition on nineteenth-century *contadino* consciousness.

Verga often layers the realistic detail of his short stories over folkoric narrative structures. He employs this strategy most strikingly in "Story of the Saint Joseph Donkey" (1881). The story is an elaboration of a traditional Italian folktale form, the animal fable or animal tale, a brief narrative of a particular animal's adventures (Calvino xx; Dégh 68). The Saint Joseph Donkey of the title is the tale's principal character, his life and death a metaphor for peasant hardship. Verga's choice of a donkey as protagonist suits the theme of peasant hardship especially well, since the peasants he depicts typically work like donkeys, the humblest, most docile, and most encumbered of the *Mezzogiorno*'s domesticated beasts (Pacifici 11). The donkey, a creature common in Italian folklore from the time and influence of storytellers like Aesop, symbolizes a number of proverbial, and in many cases, real Southern peasant values and traits: humility, obstinacy, patience, simplicity (Cooper, *Illustrated* 16). Ubiquitous in folktales of the Italian South, the donkey as protagonist made stories of their own troubles tolerable to the peasants' ears (Mangione and Morreale 35). "Story of the Saint Joseph Donkey" is then a sophisticated folktale, an authentic expression of peasant consciousness.

Like Saint Joseph Donkeys, the name for the least productive donkeys of the *Mezzogiorno*, peasants, regardless of their labors, were little valued, treated as nothing by the upper classes and government of their society, rendered mute in their resistance to authority by their inability to speak anything but a local dialect, by the power of feudal custom, and by brute force, (Viscusi, "Narrative" 80–82).[2] Adding insult to injury, a nobleman might sarcastically call a peasant *"Santu"* ("Saint"), poking fun as his saintly poverty (Covello 79). What Verga gives us then is a triple analogy—symbolic, serious, sarcastic—of donkey, peasant, saint. His story recounts the life and death of one particular Saint Joseph Donkey. The Donkey, like the peasants, is treated as a commodity: an object valued for the work he can perform, and devalued to nothingness as he is able to perform less and less work. The Donkey's breeder spends an entire day haggling his price with the Donkey's first owner, Neli.

> "It's a beautiful colt," said the owner, "and he's worth more than thirty–five *lire*. Don't pay attention to that black and white coat like a magpie's...In all honesty, I don't know where the colt got that magpie coat. But his build's good, believe me! You don't judge men by their faces. Look what a chest he's got! And those legs like pillars! Look how he holds his ears! When you have a donkey who keeps his ears that straight, you can put him to a cart or to a plow, just as you like, and make him carry four *tumoli* of buckwheat better than a mule, I swear by the holy day that's today! Feel this tail; you and your whole family could hang on it!" (Verga 149)

The breeder denies the Donkey's individuality, his "magpie coat" and its association with saintliness, to take full economic advantage of him, to have his whole family, in an economic sense, hang on the donkey's tail. In Verga's *Mezzogiorno*, you don't judge donkeys by their coats or "men by their faces." The analogy becomes clear: the breeder in his prevarication, the landowners in their control, the Donkey in his sturdiness and compliance, the peasants in their nothingness.

The analogy gains in clarity and force as the plot progresses. With each episode the Donkey becomes more of an individual, more human. As events unfold, we frequently see, hear, and feel them from the Donkey's perspective. "Meanwhile, [the Donkey] kept tripping along behind Neli, trying to bite his jacket for fun, as if he knew it was the jacket of his new owner, and as if he didn't care that he was forever leaving the stable where he had been warm beside his mother, where he had rubbed his muzzle on the edge of the manger, or had butted and capered with the ram, and had teased the pig in its little corner" (155). As the "colt" (156) and his labor change hands, he is gradually broken in both body and spirit. Eventually, he

> became so tired that he didn't even feel like biting into the pile of straw…Then he let his muzzle and his ears droop, like a full-grown donkey, his eyes lifeless, as if he were tired of looking at that vast white countryside which…seemed made only to let you die of thirst and to make you trot around on the sheaves. In the evening, he went back to the village with his saddlebags full, and the owner's boy kept pricking him in the withers, as they went along the path's hedges which seemed alive with the chirping of the titmice and the fragrance of catmint and rosemary, and the donkey would have liked to take a bite, if they hadn't made him trot all the time so that the blood went down to his legs and they had to take him to the farrier; but his owner didn't care at all, because the harvest had been good, and the colt had made his thirty-two and a half *lire*. (156)

Like a peasant child made to work in the fields, the immature Donkey is prematurely exploited and downtrodden.

Verga compares the Donkey explicitly to a human being in the episode at the farrier's, in which the Donkey "tried to break loose from the twisted rope which squeezed his lip, his eyes wild from the pain as if he were human" (157). Like the peasants, the Donkey falls further and further into misery. The narrator remarks, "And yet there are so many Christians who are no better off" than animals, the Donkey and other beasts who "shielded themselves by huddling close together" under "stars that were shining like swords," beasts whose "harness sores shuddered and quivered in the cold as if they could speak" (162). The comparison is culturally apt as well as explicit, since, in *Mezzogiorno* society of the era, men and their beasts often worked, rested, and celebrated side by side (Manoukian 17).

At story's end, the personified Donkey has suffered nearly to death. It is only then that he is given some comfort by "a poor widow, in a hut more broken down than the lime kiln itself, where the stars went through the roof like swords" (Verga 162). This old peasant woman lives under the same conditions as the Donkey, "as if she were in the open" (162); and she sees fit, despite her poverty, to care for him. The "poor Saint Joseph donkey was better off during his last days, since the widow kept him like a treasure, thanks to the money he had cost her, and at night she went to find straw and hay for him, and kept him in the hut beside her bed, where he gave off heat like a little fire; and in this world one hand washes the other" (163). Here, the widow gives care based on affection, but at least as much on economic interdependence: the dual motivation of relations among members of the peasant family. Although, for example, children were, naturally, loved by their parents and siblings, they also were expected to work with the rest of the family as soon as they were able (Alba 32). Fathers, in return, were expected to earn the lion's share of family bread; and mothers, if and when they were not working in the fields, were expected to keep household order (Gambino, *Blood* 128–182).

When the Donkey "knelt down just like the real Saint Joseph donkey in front of the Christ Child, and he didn't want to get up any more" (Verga 164), the widow and her own fever-stricken son are left without their only means of earning bread, the donkey, the one-time conveyance of the Christian world's savior. By this point in the narrative, the Donkey's treatment in death seems no worse than his treatment in life. A passerby tells the widow, "'I'm buying only the wood, because here's all the donkey's worth...'And he kicked the carcass, which sounded like a broken drum" (164). The folkloric Donkey suffers and dies, the way centuries of Southern *contadini* did, most often bound in thankless, hopeless, and endless servitude to their landowning masters, or, at best, to their own tiny pieces of land.

Yet, to this land that both sustained them and sapped their strength, peasants remained true. Life there, like the familiar folktale, was the only story they knew: not necessarily a happy one, but one from which they could draw discernable themes and learn practical lessons. While it is true that many ultimately left, driven by economic crisis and the desire to improve their condition, they did so reluctantly (Nelli 31). Their village and its surroundings, every hovel, stone, and meadow, contained all they knew of history and life (Alba 28). Their attachment to their *paesi* was a spiritual one, and at a distance, they conceived of those *paesi* as pastorals to which they would happily, must even, return.

Prior to the 1880s, Southern Italian migration meant, in most cases, movement within the Italian Peninsula. And most of the landless laborers who migrated, as was later the case with emigrants to America, were men. These men were typically *giornalieri*, day laborers. Ninety per cent of all male peasants belonged to this group (Mack Smith 149). These men moved from place to place, in pursuit of work, living away from their families most of the time (Alba 79).

Such movement for economic survival finds expression in the Sicilian version of a folktale that influenced Verga, entitled "Out in the World." It begins, "There was a widow with two daughters and a son named Peppi, who was at a loss to earn his bread. While mother and daughters were spinning one day, Peppi said, 'Listen, Mother; with your leave, I am going out into the world'" (Calvino 616). Peppi represents the young, unmarried men who made up seventy-five per cent of emigrants from *Mezzogiorno* towns (Archdeacon 139; Douglass 101). Once out in the world, he works at first for room and board, and seeks money only in order to return to his family. He pleads with the landowner for whom he labors, "Carnival is coming, and you couldn't give me a little money just this one time so I could go and celebrate with my mother and sisters?" (Calvino 617). The landowner refuses to remunerate labor, a problem for Peppi, but an absolute barrier to upward mobility for late nineteenth-century peasants caught between feudalism and capitalism (Douglass 35–36; Mack Smith 148–57; Nelli 22–23), victims of the *Mezzogiorno*'s near exclusion from the emerging international capitalist economy (Alba 38). While the Southern landowners themselves generally did not have enough capital to transform their *latifondia* from subsistence to market operations (Mack Smith 151), the landless Southern peasant could not even imagine such operations.

The solution for Peppi is a sly, "tough" (Calvino 618), anthropomorphic ox, a symbol of peasant *furberia,* cleverness, and perseverence. The ox instructs Peppi to ask the master, who hates the ox, to give him to Peppi in place of money, which the master does. One day, Peppi hears a proclamation: "WHOEVER FEELS UP TO PLOWING FIFTY ACRES OF LAND IN ONE DAY'S TIME WILL RECEIVE THE KING'S DAUGHTER IN MARRIAGE; OR, IN THE EVENT HE'S ALREADY MARRIED, TWO PILES OF GOLD. BUT WHOEVER TRIES AND FAILS, DIES" (618). Peppi and the ox succeed in plowing fifty acres of land in a single day. The king is reluctant to marry his noble daughter to "that ugly peasant" (619), so he asks Peppi, "'What do you want, two piles of gold coins?'" To which Peppi replies, "'I'm a bachelor, Majesty. What would I do with gold pieces? I've come for my wife'" (619). Once the king agrees, Peppi endears himself by slaughtering the ox, as the ox instructs him, for the wedding feast. Peppi kills off the symbol of his servitude, whose magical hoof causes his matrimonial bedchamber to grow "full of flowers and fruit out of season" (620). Peppi himself, a peasant at heart, is himself out of season as a noble living in a castle.

Peppi's solution to poverty is characteristic of the folktale, with its pre-capitalistic sensibility (Propp 17). It is a solution that relies still on the graces of the *galantuomini*. Such a solution was an unlikely one for the real peasants of the *Mezzogiorno*; and for Peppi it is only temporary. After his wedding, his sisters and brothers-in-law conspire to rob him of his money, by exploiting his trust. They learn the secret of his fertility from his wife, wager him that they know it, and when they win the wager, literally send him packing, "set out dressed as a peasant and carrying his knapsack" (Calvino 621).

Only Peppi's initiative and his curiosity restore him to his fortune and wife. He goes off in quest of the Sun, through a series of fantastic feats comes to speak with it, and bargains with it to set at an unusual hour, so that he can win back his possessions from his in-laws, as they had done from him. Upon winning this second wager, Peppi initially refuses his reward, announcing to the court, "'I intend to show you the heart of a peasant'—as they still called him...'I have no desire for the property of others, but only for my own'" (622). When the king hears this, he "insisted on embracing [Peppi] and, removing his crown, placed it on Peppi's head...So goes the story of Peppi, who started out as a starving cowherd and ended up the wealthiest and happiest of kings" (622). Peppi renounces property gained through trickery, and ultimately gains it through humility and abstinence, enacting the values and virtues practical only in the Italy of a folktale. A more realistic portrayal of values, but still not representative of reality, is Mazzarò's obsessive acquisition of property in Verga's "Property." Of course, Mazzarò's degree of success would have been nearly as rare for a peasant as Peppi's crown.

Like Verga's tales "Out in the World," then, illustrates the peasant virtues of hard work, humility, initiative, perseverance, but it does not offer a realistic solution to peasant problems. That solution could exist only outside of the society in which such tales were widely told. It would be left to the peasants who took part in the great emigration of the late nineteenth and early twentieth centuries; who, although they did not share Peppi's means, shared his values and virtues.

The actual peasants who became the great emigration were not of the lowest economic class. They were those peasants who feared falling into the abyss of poverty, *spinti,* driven, or, literally, pushed, to improve their lot. As one American official of the era stated, "One of the complaints of the present day of the Italian officials is that the very best young blood of the Italian plebes is going out of the country. They recognize that fact. It is the man with the initiative who leaves" (McLaughlin qtd in Nelli 33). In danger of being driven over the brink of indigence by a rash of economic disasters—the unfair redistribution of lands and the dissolution of feudal ties, combined with the effects of extended drought, pervasive phylloxera, overproduction of agricultural products (especially wine and wheat), burdensome taxes, and the restrictive agricultural trade policies of the Italian government—nearly twenty million Italians, full of hope for a brighter economic future, emigrated (from 1861 to 1940) from an Italy that in 1901 contained a population of only thirty-three million (Sori 19). Most of these young men planned to return and buy pieces of their native soil. Most of the immigrants to the United States, ninety percent of whom came from the *Mezzogiorno* (Nelli 32), had never ventured beyond their villages. When they arrived in America, they found themselves alone or with just a few people who spoke their language. Most often, they were illiterate.

As the immigrants who remained in the New World—approximately half of those who came (Archdeacon 137–140)—would discover, literacy in English, at least a degree of literacy, was tantamount to success in America. Understandably, the trope of literacy is central to Italian immigrant autobiography. To understand why the autobiographers held literacy out as a symbol of success in early twentieth-century America, one needs to understand that in the United States, then as now, productivity depended upon oral and written communication. Such was not necessarily the case in Italy, where in 1901, the illiteracy rate was 70 per cent in Campania, 69.5 per cent in Apulia, 75.4 per cent in Basilicata, 78.7 per cent in Calabria, and 70.9 per cent in Sicily (Covello 246).

A problem for the Italian immigrants, the "birds of passage"—so-called by Americans, most of whom did not believe they could assimilate (Alba 40)—were the vast and many differences between the two societies of which they would take part: Post-Risorgimento Italy and Gilded Age/Progressive Era America. The peasants came from a rural, feudal, rigidly stratified society governed by unwritten, traditional laws of community and local allegiances. They arrived in an increasingly urban, capitalistic, mobile society governed, at least in theory, by official legislation. Their dilemma is crystallized in a sentence from Robert Viscusi's 1995 novel, *Astoria.* "A whole nation walked out of the middle ages, slept in the ocean, and awakened in New York in the twentieth century" (22).

Although it contradicts the Italian government's official encouragement of emigration during the period in question, "Gli emigranti," by Emilio Salgari (1863–1911), a newspaper account of the immigrants' passage to America, provides a telling Italian perspective on the great journey to a new life.

> Many times you have heard talk of those poor peasants who, without means of earning their bread in their own little *paesi*, go to seek their fortune in distant America, and perhaps you have seen many of them depart, crowding onto train cars, carrying their few rags, their last bit of wealth. Those wretches, before reaching America, must cross an immense ocean, the Atlantic, and travel twenty-five days, sometimes thirty, aboardship.
>
> We present to you now a scene of emigration. Look at all those peasants, who have abandoned our beautiful Italy, gathered together in the hold of a ship. With them are their women and children.
>
> It's dinnertime. All crowd around the cooks and the sailors to receive their bowls of soup. But the ocean is not calm, and the ship, tossed by the waves, bounces around wildly, jostling everyone.
>
> The bowls overturn, children fall to the floor, losing their soup, others cling to their mommies' skirts and howl with fright, or they are helped by their older brothers and sisters, while the parents run back and forth, everywhere, for fear of going without dinner.
>
> At sea, these are everyday occurrences, scenes played out over and over again, which try the patience and the hunger of those poor peasants.
>
> But finally, the ocean crossed, the coastline of America is in sight, they debark onto those distant shores. But how many disillusionments often await them there, and how many return to their fatherland poorer than they left! (translation mine) (Savana and Straniero 341)

Given the trauma of the their experience, we can easily understand how the emigrants might have come to idealize life in Italy, the familiar, even as they made their way in the Italian colonies of America.

Chapter 2

AMERICANS IN THE (UN)MAKING: AMERICAN IMAGES OF ITALIAN AMERICAN MEN AND THE *IMPRESA/RIPRESA* OF ITALIAN IMMIGRANT AUTOBIOGRAPHY

Nearly seventy-five percent of Italian immigrants to the United States during the period 1890–1930 were men (Archdeacon 139), most of them young and unskilled. The preponderance of young men among the immigrants made it easier for American nativists to paint Italians as a menace to Anglo American life, as *The New York Times* did, following the 1891 lynchings of eleven innocent Italian immigrant men by a vigilante New Orleans mob. The mob had suspected the Italians of murdering police captain David Hennessy, whose last words were, "The dagoes did it," and had taken the law into its own hands. Although a *Times* editorial condemned murder as a solution to the problem in New Orleans, it justified the mob's actions, concluding, "These sneaking and cowardly Sicilians, the descendants of bandits and assassins, who have transported to this country the lawless passions, the cut-throat practices, the oath-bound societies of their native country, are to us a pest without mitigation." (qtd. in Iorizzo and Mondello 85).

During the early years of the twentieth century, such nativistic attitudes held sway; while they did, Peter Patelli, my great-grandfather, lived very much apart from American society. With his artisan training, he found work at a Manhattan construction site, but returned every evening to his predominantly Italian Brooklyn neighborhood, where he could speak his dialect as well as standard Italian, and eat an American version of familiar food. He lived alone in a small apartment, among the other Italian immigrants to this community, and rarely interacted with English speakers.

Peter arrived in America before 1917. That same year a twenty-year campaign for a literacy test designed to curb the flow of unlettered immigrants, a campaign led by restriction activists Prescott Hall and Robert DeCourcy Ward, bore fruit (Curran 120). Congress made the test law part of the 1917 Immigration Restriction Act (one of many passed from the 1880s to the 1920s). Yet, even if my great-grandfather had arrived in 1918, his illiteracy in English likely would not have barred his entry, since, during World War I and for several years afterward, big business's demand for cheap immigrant labor guaranteed that any new restrictions would often be relaxed in practice (128). Only after the returning soldiers were fully re-integrated in the United States economy, would Congress pass the Immigration Restriction Act of 1924, the so-called "Quota" or "National Origins" Act, which achieved restrictionist goals as previous acts had not, limiting to 150,000 per year the number of European immigrants to America, and limiting each national group to a percentage of this number based on their percentage of the United States population as recorded by the 1890 census (Higham 317–30).

Although he had arrived in time, as long as Peter remained illiterate in English, he could not move up to a supervisory position in a construction company, a reality that compelled him to learn English. He made an effort to speak with his non-Italian co-workers. He began patronizing shops beyond his Italian enclave, striking up conversation with clerks and other customers. In a Lower East Side Manhattan candy store, he bought *The New York Times,* reading it everyday, as best he could, until he could read it cover to cover in one evening. As soon as he had gained a command of the language, a construction site superintendent, noticing that Peter could speak both English and Italian, and, on top of that, could read and write well, promoted him to foreman of a crew. Soon after, my great-grandfather left the company to start one of his own, with the help of one Mr. Wilson—to this day, I have never heard anyone in the family call him by his first name—an American friend and backer. Soon after that, he met and married an Italian American woman, whose grandmother had been a sharpshooter in Wild West shows traveling America in the 1880s. Peter had by now completely arrived in his new country.

Years later, by the time he had done well enough to fulfill his dream of living again in Italy, he had made too many commitments here—to an American-born wife and children, and to employees and clients who relied on his business—ever to return to the medieval hill town of his youth, which his mind, through years of American toil, had transformed into a site of pastoral beauty, timeless contentment. Other immigrants also remembered their towns as pastoral places, but, more than Peter, contrasted their pastorals with visions of America as money-driven brave new world devoid of the traditions and values that made life worth living.

Some seventy percent of the great wave of Italian immigrants to the United States were *contadini* from the *Mezzogiorno* (Vecoli 259). In the middle of the nineteenth century, the Risorgimento came and passed them by. Following unification, the urban forces of the North and South worked in tandem to establish a protectionist economic regime under which the *Mezzogiorno* became, in essence, a colony of the North, subjugated by force and political chicanery (Gramsci 94). This chicanery continued from the time of the Risorgimento through the reign of Mussolini (and, some would say, continues today), and fostered an attitude of suspicion and aloofness from authority and outsiders, which immigrants took with them to the New World.

In the year 1900, more than eighty percent of Italians still worked the land for a living (Iorizzo and Mondello 56). In the face of adverse government policy, ongoing absentee landlordism, and the perpetual difficulties of sharecropping or squeezing a living out of inadequate land holdings, over four million Italians left for the United States between 1880 and 1920 (Nelli 41). Emigration to America had to be especially difficult for men who had relied on their village communities and members of their families to survive both "regimes that were as destructive natural disasters" (Glazer and Moynihan 184) and natural disasters themselves. Add to these woes the need to leave behind their betrothed or wives, children, families, and the fields of Italy, for the squalor and loneliness of ghettoes and industrial labor, and it is easy to understand the tendency of Italian immigrant men either to return to Italy, as "birds of passage," during times of low demand for immigrant labor, or, if they remained in America, to develop a nostalgia for Italian life. The vast majority of Italian men who immigrated to American wound up in American cities, in occupations that alienated them from the land. The 1900 census revealed that most of these men worked in personal and domestic service, transportation and trade, and manufacturing and mining, not in agriculture (Iorizzo and Mondello 60).

These immigrants began to feel a sense of dislocation that speaks to the comments of one American observer who, in 1881, remarked, "The idyllic life of an Italian hillside or of a dreaming medieval town is but poor preparation for the hand-to-hand struggle for bread of an overcrowded city" (qtd. in Iorizzo and Mondello 78). Although their lives in Italy had usually been far from "idyllic," those lives became so in the immigrant men's memories; memories set to pastoralizing Italy,[1] not only by the difficulty of their lives in America, but also by the symbiotic forces of nativism and misrepresentation of Italians and Italian Americans in American popular literature and culture.

Literary portraits of Italian American men and boys as libertines, criminal beasts, buffoons, or musical waifs fostered the nativistic climate of Guilded Age and Progressive Era America, and flourished in it. Although writers like James Fenimore Cooper and Nathaniel Hawthorne expressed admiration for Italy and Italians (albeit mingled with moral condescension and exoticism), later writers like Mark Twain—who once wrote that Italians were "strangers to cleanliness" (DeConde 137)—and Henry James—especially in his account of mute Italian immigrant ditch-diggers "of the superlatively southern type," in *The American Scene* (qtd. in Boelhower, *Through* 21)—usually expressed contempt for them.

Twain and James were hardly, however, the era's principal purveyors of unsavory Italian American characters. William Dean Howells, who often included rounded, admirable Italian characters in his fiction, nonetheless also included Italian characters who are noble savage types common in the Anglo American literary tradition (Russo 59). Later, lesser literary lights such as the dialect poet Thomas A. Daley and novelist Samuel Ornitz perpetuated Italian stereotypes. Ornitz's 1923 novel *Haunch, Paunch, and Jowl*, a satirical rags-to-riches saga populated with ethnic Americans, includes an Italian American ne'er-do-well known only as "Dago Jack." Daley, for his part, published several volumes of Italian immigrant dialect poems in his lifetime, the most popular of which was 1919's *McAroni Ballads*. Gaetano Cipolla claims that Daley's work is important because it presents Italian Americans as "humane and interesting" people. Until the publication of *McAroni Ballads*, Cipolla contends, an American public subject to the spoutings of pseudo-scientific eugenicists, was not used to perceiving Italian Americans as either humane or interesting (46).

Unfortunately, the laughable typography, diction, and rhyme of Daley's work contradict Cipolla's favorable reading, as this passage from the 1906 poem "Handicapped" shows.

> Eef I could talka 'Merican
> Like w'at I can Italian,
> So stronga langwadge eet would be
> You would be scare'to joke weeth me.
> Een Italy I am so queeck
> For theenk of sassy theengs to speak,

W'en som'wan makin'fun weeth me,
Dat nexta time dey let me be.
Da professori from da school
Som'time was try for mak'me fool;
Ah! wal, they find, you bat my life,
My tongue ees sharpa like da knife.
(qtd. in Cipolla 47)

Daley is clearly engaging here in romantic primitivism (Russo 52) in his depiction of an Italian immigrant man with a noble soul but a savage tongue—which, in Italian, by the way, is "sharpa like da knife." Is the vaguely criminal metaphor an accident? Not likely in an era that began with an 1891 *Times*-sanctioned mob lynching of Italian immigrants in New Orleans, sustained a eugenicist school of social theory, and ended with the 1924 passage of the "National Origins" Immigration Restriction Act. Like the language of African American dialect poetry of the day, the language of Daley's poems tends to dehumanize its subjects, rendering them acceptable targets for verbal, social, and physical abuse.

If Daley's work had a negative effect on the public image of Italian American men, the work of more popular writers had an earlier, more lasting, and more profound effect on that image. Two of the more pernicious distortions of Italian American male selfhood are O. Henry's short story, "The Coming Out of Maggie," from the author's second collection, *The Four Million,* and Horatio Alger's *Phil, the Fiddler, or, The Story of a Young Street Musician* (1872). *The Four Million,* published in 1906, contains stories such as "The Gift of the Magi," which had earlier been published in large-circulation magazines and newspapers of the time, including *The New York World, The Smart Set,* and *McClure's*. In this form and between hard covers, O. Henry's stories, like Alger's novel, reached millions of Americans (Litz 394).

As many of O. Henry's New York stories do, "The Coming Out of Maggie" portrays the working class, particularly the Irish and Italian American working class. Its plot demonstrates O. Henry's technique of manipulating ideas and sentiments already in the era's cultural air (Van Doren, qtd. in Litz 395). The story reinforces the then current image of the Italian man as seductive, dangerous criminal by nature. The setting is an eventful night in the life of Maggie Toole, a young Irish girl of "dull eyes, broad mouth and left-handed style of footwork in the two-step" (O. Henry 69). To the surprise of everyone at the Lower East Side Irish Clover Leaf Social Club, Maggie arrives at a Club dance escorted by a handsome young man who calls himself "Terry O'Sullivan." The Irish lads at the dance note that "Terry" puts on "Beau Brummel airs" (72). The narrator tells us—alluding to Hawthorne's Donatello—that Terry "danced like a faun; he introduced manner and style and atmosphere; his words came trippingly upon his tongue" (74).

In the end, Terry is revealed to be no Irishman at all. "You ain't no O'Sullivan," exclaims Dempsey Donovan, who will eventually rescue Maggie from the threat of miscegenation, as well as recognize her charms himself, "You are a ring-tailed monkey" (77). The "monkey," we discover, is really Tony Spinelli, a local Italian youth, who, upon being discovered and challenged to a fistfight by Dempsey, with "a murderous look in his dark eyes" pulls "a long, bright stiletto" "from his bosom" (79), which Maggie manages to knock away. Foiled, Tony flees the dance, but not before he "hissed" (like a serpent) "something unintelligible" (Italian?) "between his teeth" (79). Dempsey calls Tony a "cheese slicer" and a "Guinea"; Maggie admits, "I knew there'd be nothin'doin'for him if he came as a Dago"; and Dempsey summarily explains, "Them Guineas always carries knives," before the two members of the more established immigrant group go off happily together.

O. Henry's story reflects and feeds the early twentieth-century growth of nativistic, racist prejudice against Italians, who were coming to America in rapidly increasing numbers. More importantly, it and other literature that caricatures Italian men perpetuated one of many stereotypes that Italian immigrant men of the period had (and Italian American men have since had) to overcome: the ruthless criminal. In a 1909 issue of *Harper's Weekly*, Frank Marshall White writes, "Though we do not know even approximately the number of Italian criminals in the United States, what we do know, nevertheless, [is] that they have piled up a record of crime here during the last ten years that is unparalleled in the history of a civilized country in time of peace" (qtd. in LaGumina 93). White goes on to lament, "During the entire period in which exotic malefactors have been swarming into the country, nothing of any value has been done to stem the tide" (93). White's alarmist comments found support in the pseudo-scientific eugenics of the period.

During the early part of the century, working class Americans, fed a steady diet of propaganda by the commercial, journalistic, and intellectual establishment, grew to perceive Italians and other Southern and Eastern Europeans as racially inferior beings (Curran 116). In his 1914 treatise, *The*

Old World in the New: The Significance of Past and Present Immigration to the American People, renowned professor of sociology and staunch nativist Edward Alsworth Ross distinguishes by differences in the size and shape of their heads the "North Italian" race from the "South Italian," the latter of which group, for their numbers and nature, he sees as the greatest threat to "Nordic" American civilization (97). Ross goes on to claim, "In nothing are the two peoples so unlike as in their crimes. While northern Italy leads in fraud and chicane, southern Italy reveals a rank growth of the ferocious crime that goes with a primitive stage of civilization. The contrast is between force and fraud, violence and cunning" (100–101). "In homicide, rape, blackmail, and kidnapping [Italian immigrants] lead the foreign born" (106).

During the period of O. Henry's and Ross's greatest fame, the "luck and pluck" novels of Horatio Alger were enjoying unprecedented popularity, a fact attributable as much to the need to assimilate record numbers of young male immigrants arriving in American cities, as to the acceleration of industrialization and urbanization. More copies of Alger's boy books sold between the author's death in 1899 and 1920 than had in his lifetime (Decker 1). Jeffrey Decker and other scholars before him find nativistic attitudes inherent in novels such as *Ragged Dick*, but it is unlikely that Alger intended his only story of Italian immigrant life, *Phil, the Fiddler*, to reinforce nativistic stereotypes of Italians—although this is an effect it likely had thirty years after its original publication.

In the years following the Civil War, Alger worked in conjunction with Giovanni Secchi de Casale, editor of *Eco d'Italia*, the Italian American daily, to investigate the *padrone* system as it operated in New York's Little Italy (Gardner 207–226). *Padroni* were Italian agents working on behalf of Italian shipping lines and American businesses, most of whom spoke English, who recruited and sponsored men and boys from Italy, paid or supplemented the cost of their passage, and found them work in America once they arrived. In return, the immigrant workers would either pay the *padroni* a percentage of their earnings, work for employers who kicked money back to the *padroni*, or live in overpriced boarding houses that did the same. Often, the *padrone* system kept young children like Alger's fictional Phil working in the streets under conditions of virtual slavery. Secchi de Casale's tireless newspaper campaign and the publication of *Phil, the Fiddler* helped force passage of a state law creating the Society for the Prevention of Cruelty to Children (225–26). In 1872, before the great wave of Italian immigration brought a perceived Italian menace, Italian immigrants, especially boys, made acceptable charity cases, and, sometimes, in the world of fiction, sympathetic characters. It is, in fact, the Irish Mickey Maguire, of *Ragged Dick* and other novels, as a representative of a more assimilated immigrant group, who plays Alger's villain.

Whatever Alger's intention, *Phil, the Fiddler* is a story that could have left only a negative impression of Italian males on at least two generations of American minds. The story follows the trials and triumphs of Phil, a twelve year-old Italian boy fiddler, who is sold into "a form of chattel slavery" (Fink v) by his father, the narrative's first unscrupulous Italian man. Phil is then sent to live and work in New York for a *padrone.* Undoubtedly, many *padroni,* such as Phil's, exploited and abused the immigrants who relied on them for direction (Phipard 470), but most had at least some beneficial effect, in several ways (Iorizzo and Mondello 166). They not only helped Italians to come to America, where their economic prospects were surely better than they would have been in Italy, but they also directed those who came to work sites across the nation, ensuring a widespread and enduring Italian American presence. Often, they represented the only means of escape from Italian immigrant ghettoes like the Little Italy in which Phil's *padrone* attempts to hold him prisoner (Iorizzo and Mondello 164–183).

This mixed blessings of the *padrone* system contradict the biases of Alger's novel, as does its relatively rapid decline. The passage of time obviated the system, as immigrants gained a firm foothold and were thus able to assist others in journeying and settling in America. By the time *Phil, the Fiddler* was reprinted in 1906, the *padroni* had virtually ceased to function as immigration agents. Alger's doctrinaire novel, however, continued to portray as current their former effect on child laborers in a neighborhood of New York that was no longer as crowded and squalid as it had been three decades earlier. The narrator of *Phil* declares,

> What wonder that the boys sold into such cruel slavery should be estranged from the fathers who for a few paltry ducats sell the liberty and happiness of their children! Even where the contract is for a limited term of years, the boys in five cases out of ten are not returned at the appointed time. A part, unable to bear the hardships and privations of the life upon which they enter, are swept off by death, while of those that survive, a part are weaned from their homes, or are not permitted to go back. (45)

Phil and the other Italian boys in the novel suffer at the hands of the evil *padrone*, an "oppressive task master" (17), "a short man, very dark, with fierce black eyes, and a sinister countenance" (31), a "tyrant" (109) whose "dark face was marked by an expression of greed" (66). To go along with his dark "sinister countenance," the *padrone* has "one of those hard, cruel natures that delight in inflicting pain and anguish upon others" (68). In sum, he is a swarthy Italian beast bent on making his charges'lives miserable for his own profit and pleasure.

The *padrone* beats Phil and the other boys if they do not bring home what he considers a sufficient day's earnings, which he keeps for himself, to indulge his taste for alcohol (33) and other vices. Alger beats this point to death on every other page. That the *padrone* has such vices, and that Alger harps on them, only served to fix in the minds of Progressive Era readers stereotypes of Italian men: the sorts of stereotypes created and promulgated by nativist intellectuals like Ross who notes (in a passage on Italians subtitled "CHARACTERISTIC VICES," from *The Old World in the New*) that "in the Italian home the bottle of 'rock and rye' is seen with increasing frequency"; that "Italians...are addicted to gambling. Games of chance flourish in their saloons"; and that "many a knife-thrust has come out of a game of cards" (105).

Unfortunately, the *padrone* is *Phil, the Fiddler*'s only adult Italian male character other than Phil's absent father, the man who has sold his son into slavery (30). As Phil flees Manhattan, in an attempt to escape his taskmaster, the cruel stepfather figure's "sharp eyes" (68) and presence loom, and his reach in the form of spies and lieutenants constantly threatens the fugitive Phil with falling "into the power of that old brute again" (178). Readers of Alger's novel, especially young readers, were left with frightening images of a foreign monster.

The other prominent Italian American male in the book is a child, Phil himself, the exotic musical waif, the "dark-eyed Italian boy" of "brilliant brown complexion" (50). He is "twelve years old, but small of his age." His face, "[i]n spite of the dirt, is "strikingly handsome, especially when lighted up by a smile" (9). His voice is "clear and melodious" as he sings "with so much feeling that the effect was agreeable" (13). Phil is another Italian faun, another Faunus (or Pan) of American literature, an echo of Hawthorne's or James's handsome Italian boys, this one available to a wide and impressionable readership.

To Alger's audience, Phil was an exotic jewel and a fatherless child, a protagonist extremely appealing to paternalistic, middle- and upper-class Progressive Era Americans, who often viewed immigrants as passive entities ripe and ready to receive American beneficence and re-education (Higham 119). Even Jane Addams, who preached respect for immigrant customs, on occasion and in a patronizing tone, expressed the prevailing idea that immigrants would be better off adopting American ways. In *Twenty Years at Hull House,* she writes, "They come to us with their petty lawsuits, sad relics of the *vendetta*, with their incorrigible boys, with their hospital cases, with their aspirations for American clothes, and with their needs for an interpreter" (170). Like Jane Addams' charges, Phil, although he has something of the Old World to contribute to American life—his music, the gift of the shepherd boy's patron god—is destined for American shepherding.

Phil's American shepherd appears in the person of Doctor Drayton, a physician who, at story's end, discovers Phil half-frozen in a snowstorm, and adopts him. Plucky and lucky, having displayed the gumption to strike out on his own, having learned English well, having "been fortunate in securing a good home," Phil is assured success and satisfaction. We learn that "[s]ome years hence the doctor promises to give himself a vacation, and take Phil with him to Europe, where he will seek out his Italian home, and his mother with whom he has already opened communication by letter. So we leave Phil in good hands, and with the prospect of a prosperous career" (264). Through his strength of character and diligence, Phil becomes a successful American; and it is Phil's success that will enable him to revisit Italy, a land that he, like other immigrants *in absentia*, believes to be a pastoral land of "olive-trees and orange-trees and grapes," "much nicer" than America (45).

Throughout the narrative, "[Phil] had been dreaming of his mother and his far-off Italian home" while living "the harsh realities of life" (100) in America. Middle- and upper-class American readers might have tolerated (or missed) this and other off-hand criticism of American life throughout the novel, because Phil's story unfolds in a setting—an immigrant slum in New York—foreign (in all senses) to them. They might also have tolerated such criticism, because Phil's story remains essentially a rags-to-riches tale, in which Alger does his due diligence to capture, in exotic hues, the American myth of the self-made man. Finally, readers of the period could rest assured that Phil would return to Italy "in good hands," on "vacation," understandably wanting to visit his mother—the Doctor makes clear that Phil "has found" an American "father" (263)—and wanting, in James's words, "to gaze upon certain of the highest achievements of human power" (qtd. in DeConde 132) as well as the beautiful fields of the *Bel Paese*. Like Hawthorne's artists, Phil will come to understand Italy as a garden that time has left behind. Alger's wild Italian faun will be remade a civilized American man.

Rocco Corresca takes cues from Horatio Alger in his pioneering development of complex, fully human Italian American male selves. During the nineteenth century, a handful of Italian men published Italian-language narratives of their travels to America. These include Giovanni Capellini's *Ricordi di un viaggio scientifico nell'America nel MDCCCLXIII* (1867), Carlo Gardini's *Gli Stati Uniti* (1891), and Ferdinando Fontana's *Viaggi* (1893), the last of which includes a deeply personal account of Fontana's first encounter with New York. The first English-language account of an Italian man's immigrant experience is Corresca's "The Biography of a Bootblack," which appeared in the December 4th, 1902 issue of *The Independent*. The piece's title obviously alludes to Alger's *Ragged Dick; or Street Life with the Bootblacks*. Predictably, "The Biography" tells a rags-to-riches story.

It begins with a description of Corresca's life in an Italian orphanage. We find young Rocco, like Phil, without Italian parents, ripe for American influence but attached to his native Italy. He remembers the Italian orphanage where he stays as "a good place, situated on the side of the mountain, where grapes were growing and melons and oranges and plums" (2863)—a pastoral setting, like the Italy Alger's Phil recalls. From this bucolic scene, Corresca is taken to Naples by an old man claiming to be his grandfather. This "grandfather," Corresca tells us, turns out to be a *padrone*, the first of two for whom he is forced to work. Corresca flees the *padrone*, and passes another idyllic period in the company of a kindly fisherman and his beautiful daughter, until the fisherman can no longer afford to pay him. Although Corresca's *padrone* is nearly as callous as Phil's, he does not hunt the fugitive Corresca down. In this way he is a turn-of-the-century improvement on the Alger's image of the Italian American man.

Impoverished, Corresca leaves for America, "a far off country where everybody was rich," where "Italians went...and made plenty of money, so that they could return to Italy and live in pleasure ever after" (2864). This double desire, to succeed in America (to become and rich and literate enough to tell about it) and to return to Italy "and live in pleasure ever after," defines the male selves of Italian American autobiographies throughout the early twentieth century.

Corresca reaches America by contracting with a second *padrone*, Bartolo. In America, Corresca's experiences with Bartolo echo Phil's experience with his *padrone*, but differ in several important ways. Corresca's *padrone* keeps him by contract, not by brute force. He feeds Corresca and the other boys well, telling them, "I am too kind a man, that is why I am poor." Even though he later admits he "is now a very rich man," the *padrone* does not squander money on his vices in the manner of Phil's *padrone*.

Like Phil, Corresca one day travels to Newark, not in flight, but in quest of money that he would not have to share with Bartolo. Bartolo pursues him, but is easily deterred—like Corresca's first *padrone*, he is hardly a menacing presence. In fact, in the character of this second *padrone,* Corresca presented readers of the day with an image of Italian man as complex human being, who grows rich from child labor, but at the same time acts kindly toward the immigrant boys he sponsors. Instead of responding with the threat of violence to their breaking the *padrone*/immigrant contract, Bartolo simply goes away, complaining to police that "there was no justice in this country" (2866). A good number of American readers of the time might actually have identified with him.

The most complex character of "The Biography" is Corresca himself. Unlike Phil, whose story is told from an approximation of Alger's point of view, Corresca organizes his own experiences from his own point of view. Corresca's creating his own metaphor of an Italian American male self,[2] taken in context of Gilded Age and Progressive Era distortions, amounts to a declaration of Italian American literary independence. For the first time, American readers could gain a sense of Italian American male consciousness as constructed and presented by an Italian American writer.

Corresca's "Biography" constructs an Italian American self-conscious both of economic success and, naturally for an immigrant, of his ethnic heritage. Corresca makes clear that his success is more pluck than luck, a matter of diligence and design in the manner of Benjamin Franklin, whose autobiography, by the turn of the twentieth century, had become a model American success story (Holte, "Benjamin Franklin" 101). Corresca writes,

> When the Newark boss told us that there was no more work Francisco and I talked about what we would do and we went back to Brooklyn to a saloon near Hamilton

> Ferry, where we got a job cleaning it out and slept in a little room upstairs. There was a bootblack named Michael on the corner and when I had time I helped him and learned the business. Francisco cooked the lunch in the saloon and he, too, worked for the bootblack and we were soon able to make the best polish. (2866)

Here is Franklin's apprenticeship recast.

> Then we thought we would go into business and we got a basement on Hamilton avenue [sic] near the Ferry, and put four chairs in it. We paid $75 for the chairs and all the other things...Outside we had a big sign that said:
>
> THE BEST SHINE FOR TEN CENTS
>
> Men that did not want to pay ten cents could get a good shine for five cents, but it was not an oil shine.
>
> We had two boys helping us and paid each of them fifty cents a day. The rent of the place was $20 a month, so the expenses were very great, but we made money from the beginning. We slept in the basement, but got our meals in the saloon till we could put a stove in our place, and then Francisco cooked for us all.

Here Corresca keeps Franklinesque account of his finances.

> That would not do, tho [sic], because some of our customers said that they did not like to smell garlic and onions and red herrings. I thought that was strange, but we had to do what the customers said. So we got the woman who lived upstairs to give us our meals and paid her $1.50 a week each. She gave the boys soup in the middle of the day—five cents for two plates...We had said that when we saved $1,000 each we would go back to Italy and buy a farm, but now that the time is coming we are so busy and making so much money that we think we will stay. We have opened another parlor near South Ferry, in New York. We have to pay $30 a month rent, but the business is very good. The boys in the place charge sixty cents a day because there is so much work. (2866–67)

The narrative not only demonstrates the nineteen year-old Corresca's ability to define his life, but also at times to comment on small matters of culture, such as American neighbors' negative reaction to "garlic and onions and red herrings," which he labels "strange."

The passage also reveals Corresca's sense of *Italianità*, his sense of difference from Anglo and other non-Italian Americans. At one point, he comments on antagonistic with another large ethnic group. "There are some good Irishmen," he claims, "but many of them insult Italians. They call us Dagoes" (2867). At another point, Corresca notes, "There are here plenty of Protestants who are heretics, but they have a religion, too. Many of the finest churches are Protestant, but they have no saints and no altars, which seems strange...These people are without a king such as ours in Italy. It is what they call a Republic, as Garibaldi wanted" (2867). This passage is notable for a few reasons. Even though it is written in English, it appears to be written for an Italian or Italian immigrant audience unfamiliar with American politics and American religion. Up to this point, Corresca has addressed the narrative, filled with information about Italy and constructed on the design of the American rags-to-riches tales of Franklin and Alger, to "the model reader" of immigrant autobiography, the Anglo American (Gardaphè, *Italian* 48). Finally, like many of the immigrant autobiographies that follow it, Corresca's offers both explicit and implicit criticism of American society.

Italian American immigrant autobiographers after Corresca also employ this strategy of addressing both the model reader and the Italian (American) reader who might follow the autobiographer's example. This double address allows the narrators to identify with sympathetic Americans like Corresca's first boss in Newark, while expressing their sense of ethnic difference. Their dual identification represents the starting point of Italian American selfhood in literature, the central conflict of Italian American ethnic consciousness, as Corresca and other, later Italian American narrators express it. This conflicted narrative relationship to Italian and American audiences, to Italian and American culture, to Italian and American models, is an important manifestation of *impresa/ripresa* tension.

Zingarelli's *Nuovo Vocabolario* defines *"impresa"* and *"rirpesa"* as follows:

> Impresa: *s. f.* 1. *Opera, azione che si comincia o si ha in animo di fare.* 2. *Azione, attività di una certa difficoltà e importanza, ma spesso di esito dubbio.* 3. *Organismo che coordina prestazioni di lavoro e strumenti adeguati per il conseguimento di finalità economiche.*
>
> [n. f. 1. Work or action that is undertaken for the purpose of accomplishing some task. 2. Action, activity of a certain difficulty and importance, but often of dubious result. 3. System that coordinates labor and adequate instruments for the attainment of economic ends.]
>
> Ripresa: *s. f.* 1. *Nuovo inizio, continuazione dopo una pausa o un'interruzione.* 2. *Ricupero di vitalità, energia, intensità e simile.*
>
> [n. f. 1. New beginning, continuation after a pause or interruption. 2. Recovery of vitality, energy, intensity and the like.]

These definitions, with a similar degree of accuracy in each case, describe the Italian American struggle, my great-grandfather's in life, the immigrant autobiographers' in literature, both to accumulate wealth and reconstitute Italian culture in America.

What then is the nature of these concurrent enterprises, *impresa* and *ripresa*, and how do they function in Italian American narrative?

Impresa and *ripresa* function to develop a narrator's or character's identity, his or her self. In Italian American narratives, authors manipulate narrative language and form, in order to create selves identifying with both Anglo American culture and (a regional) Italian culture (Boelhower, "Brave" 11). *Impresa* is the process by which Italian American authors tell stories that enact the lessons of Franklin's *Autobiography*, the myth of the Making of Americans. By the Making of Americans I mean the process of Americanization, and two varieties of it, assimilation and incorporation, which contended for intellectual and political ascendancy from the Progressive Era into the 1920's. Assimilation works toward making immigrants similar to Americans in language, customs, and religion, while incorporation works toward making immigrants' cultures a part of the American scene (Panunzio, *Immigration* 254–55). One sees America as melting pot, the other as cultural mosaic. The goal of the first process is cultural homogeneity; the goal of the second is cultural pluralism. Bolstered by post-World War I nativism and calls for "100 per cent Americanization" (Higham 249), assimilation eventually became the guiding principle of immigrant re-education and would remain so through the 1950s.

The myth of the making of Americans subsumes the myth of the self-made man as portrayed in the "'luck and pluck'" fiction of Horatio Alger and others through the Progressive Era (Decker xx). Although the myth of American success has often been seen as a quest for moral perfection (Spengemann and Lundquist 503), during the early twentieth century, it had everything to do, as the amoral anti-heroes of F. Scott Fitzgerald's *The Great Gatsby* and Abraham Cahan's *The Rise of David Levinsky* illustrate, with the attainment of wealth. But apart from its moral and monetary dimensions, the American success myth is a myth of individual success, the creed of a society obsessed with individualism and adherent to the cult of the self-made man (Wyllie 13). It is also a myth that plays a large role in the narratives of individual immigrant men cut off from an Italian society concerned more with the success of the family than of the individual (Orsi, "The Fault" 138).

By contrast, *Ripresa* is the process by which Italian immigrant autobiographers criticize American life (and their literary selves' individualistic pursuit of its material rewards), by subtly comparing it to an idealized version of life in Italian villages, whose values (family, honor and respect above all) ring more communitarian than American values. *Ripresa* is the narrative opposite of *impresa:* a version of pastoral by which Italian American authors reconstitute life in Italy as an idyll. It is irrelevant that Italy is not now and has never been simply a blissful, communitarian garden (Nelli 135). Pastoral is an alchemy of memory and myth (Williams 43). Imaginary as they might be, the pastoral passages and passages of return in Italian American narratives serve to criticize by comparison the American society which narrators and characters now call home. As often as they provide critical contrast, these passages also allow narrators and characters recourse to Old World values and skills that prove keys to viable selfhood (and sometimes to material success) in the New World. In this way, through the tactics of *impresa* and *ripresa,* Italian American narrators and characters develop identities both in harmony and in contrast with American values. They become hybrids, truly Italian American.

Against Progressive Era nativism; against stereotypes of Italian men in America; in celebration of New World economic success; and from longing for an idyllic Italian life lived only in their memories, Italian immigrant autobiographers who followed Corresca continued to express the *impresa/ripresa* conflict. The two most important Italian immigrant autobiographies published prior to the Immigration Restriction Act of 1924 are Pascal D'Angelo's *Son of Italy* (1924) and Constantine Panunzio's *The Soul of an Immigrant* (1921). These are essential narrative texts, insightfully and comprehensively examined by both Boelhower (in *Immigrant Autobiography in America*) and Gardaphè (in *Italian Signs, American Streets*). As models of *impresa/ripresa,* however, these texts fall short of another autobiography published well after the severe restriction of Italian immigration. During the 1930s, when the virulent nativism of the Progressive and Post-World War I eras was waning (Higham 324–30), immigrant authors were less compelled to write assimilationist tracts. In this climate, Francesco Ventresca, in 1937, published *Personal Reminiscences of a Naturalized American.*

His story begins in Introdacqua, a small town in the Abruzzi region of Italy, which was also the hometown of Pascal D'Angelo. Ventresca writes of the town's environs, "In summer there is no end to flowers and birds...rising from the wheat fields into the heavens and delighting the toilers beneath with their ever changing symphonies from dawn to dusk" (6), a pastoral setting except in times of the drought and hunger that drive *contadini* like D'Angelo abroad (D'Angelo 17). Looking back, Ventresca ponders the effect of this "beauty spot" (1) on the natives. "All these things [the natural wonders] contribute to the temperament and to the constitution of the individual who is born and reared there: sunshine, songs, smiles, energy galore!" This aspect of his Italian childhood serves Ventresca well as an autobiographical character who possesses Yankee-like virtues. "I have not yet lost my innate and acquired spirited temperament," proclaims the author, "nor my original radiant smile, nor my inexhaustible supply of energy" (7). Ventresca self-assessment values not only pluck and industry—as Alger's novels do—but also a sunny disposition, "songs," and "smiles," Italian enhancements of a protagonist in the mold of Franklin.

Ventresca's family, unlike D'Angelo's and unlike most Italian peasant families of the day, enjoys a middle class existence. Ventresca hints, however, that were he to remain in Introdacqua, his own fortunes would surely decline. At seventeen he leaves home "for Rome and vicinity to earn some money for myself" (15). In 1891 Ventresca follows the course of millions of other Italian emigrants and sails for New York, by way of Naples, the word "*bracciante*" ("laborer") stamped on his passport (20), belying his solid education. In Chapter II, "America: The Land of Promise," Ventresca lands in New York where he eats a "*hot doggie*" and drinks his first beer. He takes care to tell readers, however, that, unlike Alger's *padrone*, "in subsequent years I never took a beer. I thought more of the nickel than the glass of beer I could get for it. And, mind you, I had not read Benjamin Franklin's autobiography yet" (24). Of course Ventresca had read Franklin by the time he committed his own story to paper.

After landing in New York on his nineteenth birthday, Ventresca works his way to Indiana, where he begins his American education, going from grade school to college graduation in eight short years. Like many other immigrant autobiographers, Ventresca places a high value on English literacy (Gardaphè 36), thinking to himself, "'I must learn English and learn it well, for I need that as a background" (49–50), which of course proves true. With the help of several American friends, he graduates, and in a chapter entitled "Climbing Higher," appears to be well on his way to American success. At this point, however, instead of turning onto a career path that will lead him deeper into American culture, such as becoming a dentist or lawyer in Chicago—both of which the narrative presents as options—Ventresca decides to become a teacher of languages: not just of Italian, but of several European languages including English which he teaches to non-English speakers. This choice leads him away from the path beaten by other (Italian) immigrant Bildungsromans.

In *Son of Italy*, Pascal D'Angelo becomes a successful English-language poet by working a series of thankless menial jobs and then, *in extremis,* miraculously gaining the acceptance of his work by an American editor. In *The Soul of an Immigrant,* Panunzio becomes a successful Protestant minister, by relying on the good graces of American friends and sponsors, by working hard in their service, and by converting to an old stock American religion. Ventresca finds success not only through American agency (education in American schools and colleges and employment in America), but also through recourse and literal return to Europe. Instead of becoming a convert to American ideology, language and culture, an assimilationist, Ventresca becomes a multiculturalist, a cosmopolite, a believer not only in American opportunity but also in "the light that Italy [and the rest of Europe] had been throwing upon the world for centuries" (67).

Soon after graduating from Valparaiso—whose Latinate name recalls the paradisiacal valley of his Italian childhood—Ventresca leaves Indiana, all his books in tow, for Europe. "I planned to spend two years in Germany and one year each in France, Italy and Spain, studying languages," he recalls, "and then return to America to teach" (71). The first stop on his grand educational tour is in fact his hometown, Introdacqua, where, now as a citizen of the intellectual world, he finds he no longer belongs in a peasant village. "The things that interested me were all Greek to them, and I began to think of other climes" (81). Ventresca figures his new identity (which he calls, after Dante, his "vita nova" (39)) in terms of languages ("Greek to them"), which he sees as passport to both success and fulfillment in "[p]oetry, prose and the drama, together with music and the fine arts...enough to keep me happy" (65). Literary texts are in fact the author's touchstones for many of the episodes that follow, including one in which he is hired to accompany a group of tourists on a night out in Paris, which includes a "peep-show" (86). The author declares, "I had come to Europe to improve my knowledge of European languages, not to take in peep-shows" (86), and compares his predicament to that of the protagonist of Jean Jacques Rousseau's *Emile, ou de l'Education.*

Using one of countless letters of recommendation he receives and reproduces in the course of the narrative, Ventresca secures a job in the French capital, taking orders for commissioned art. This job leads to other letters and other positions including translator and tour guide for American tourists, in both Paris and Rome. Ventresca describes his time in these cities, as well as his time in Germany and England, in nostalgic terms. His narrative attempts to recreate experiences of European high culture that transcend time and European national boundaries, to create a pastoral of the mind. He notes that during one meal with a group of aristocrats and intellectuals, he had the "privilege" of engaging in high-minded conversation, in English, Italian, and French. "You must remember," he reminds readers, "we are speaking of life in Europe, indeed in Rome, and before the 'democratizing?' World War" (108). Although Ventresca believes in the Allies' fight, he does so with reservation, believing correctly the European society which had produced so many artistic delights to be irrevocably changed by the war.

Ventresca's European education includes both work experience and continued study of languages and literature. He pursues course work at the University of Freiburg—even a course in the study of ancient Gothic, in which language he reproduces and from which he translates "The Lord's Prayer" for readers—and independent study, confessing, "My every thought was: Read more, learn more, live more fully and richly!" (125). Over time, this education brings him enlightenment, making him feel that "the world is not so big after all, whether it is the ocean or the English Channel that separates us" (123). It also shows him that no country, not even America, is perfect in its social justice.

In Italy and other European countries, admits Ventresca, "the monopolizers of education...are very jealous of their social status and do not want the humbler element to rise" (78). But after paying low German railway fares, he observes that in America "we have only one class [of passenger], so that the millionaire and the pauper travel in the same car and pay the same price, and we can boast all we want about the price of democracy...the man with limited means is robbed" (130). He regrets the rigidity of the Italian caste system, recalling the disappointment and disillusionment of Verga's peasants, and cheers any efforts to modernize. (Several times in the narrative, he expresses deep admiration for Mussolini, whom he calls the "savior" (234) of Italy.

This was a sentiment shared, of course, by a large number of Italian Americans in the mid-1930s (Cannistraro 6) who had left a still–feudal homeland behind.) He also identifies both with the high culture of Europe and socialistic policies of some of its nations', as well the opportunity to rise, socially and economically, in America. In describing his education, he labels himself a "self-made man" (Ventresca 133), but one whose narrative making is a matter not only of career training and industry, but also spiritual questing and intellectual enlightenment in the manner of Dante and Goethe.

The rest of the story is Ventresca's American *impresa*, an account of his success, about which he concludes, "There never was a time when a man could not use an education to advantage" (50). That Ventresca's education is largely a European education lends his narrative an element of *ripresa* unparalleled in Italian immigrant autobiography. His cultural ties to Italy do not diminish his American life. Instead, they put it in perspective, enrich it and in fact make it possible. When World War I interrupts his extremely successful career as instructor in modern languages at the University of Washington, Ventresca, at the age of forty-four, is invited to compete for the position of Official Translator in the Office of Naval Intelligence. In this and other posts, he comes to translate several sensitive war-related documents, choosing, as he sees it, to be a patriot, "a stanch American" (230), who comes into contact with a number of prominent officials including senators and admirals. An appreciation and study of the Old World leads Ventresca to the heart of power and influence in the New.

Although Ventresca finds a third way, a life of the mind, museum, and book, one that bridges cultures, his narrative reflects a heart divided between Old World and New. In the Old World he is able not only to hone his Italian, but also to gain a knowledge of other European languages, which makes his American career as an interpreter and teacher of foreign languages (and author) possible. At the same time, he idealizes the Italy of his return, from the point of view of a tourist.

> My friend and I had a characteristically Neapolitan meal with spaghetti, Roman cheese, rolled meat, tomato sauce and genuine, unadulterated wine, in a tavern but a few steps from the monastery. It was out in the country, upon a hill, surrounded by cultivated land and vineyards; seeming much closer to Heaven because of our distance from the shore of Santa Lucia (our Lake Shore Drive), because of the altitude and proximity to the monastery. (153–54)

As Boelhower claims of D'Angelo's "Happy Valley," Ventresca's rediscovered Italian countryside seems "much closer to Heaven" for its situation, which, in parentheses, he analogizes for an American audience, mimicking the language of an early twentieth-century Baedeker guidebook. Ventresca mediates among Italian culture, his own sense of *Italianità,* and his fellow Americans. His *ripresa* of Italy complements and, on occasion, positively contrasts with the bustling America he now calls home.

In chapter II, for example, the first chapter on Ventresca's life in America, the narrator describes American railroad tracks—a powerful symbol of the American belief in progress, American industry, and manifest destiny.

> From the Atlantic to the Pacific, and from Canada to Mexico, one can see not only the whole rail but also the whole bedding of ties. The Italian would say this is not a bit artistic. But the American says: "never mind your art. We want efficiency, which means the greatest returns for the least outlay." And then, it would not be fair to draw seriously a comparison between a little old country like Italy and an immense new country like the United States. (28)

But of course that's just what Ventresca is up to here, contrasting the American world of efficiency with an Italian world of beauty, yet allowing that America is "but a young nation" with "all her future ahead of her" (156).

Elsewhere in the narrative, Ventresca reprints letters he has written to the Board of Education, which demonstrate both his interest and role in American education. He also reprints letters that express pro-Mussolini sentiments, and urge American political leaders to support the territorial claims and defend the "honor of Mother Italy" (236) (Cannistraro 6), to which he remains as attached as he is to his "vita nova" in America. The allusion to Dante suggests that Ventresa's new life includes America as both a kind of heaven, and a place that separates him from his true love, Italy ("If I were given the choice to live where I pleased, I should certainly choose Florence, Italy" (150).) At one point, he is asked to sell war bonds to an Italian American group. At the podium, he extols "the blessings this great country [The U. S.] offers to an immigrant, while he is still appreciative and grateful to the land that gave him birth" (230). From both countries, he tries to "choose the gold and reject the dross" (232). He is happy to remain an Italian at heart, but also proud of being a "naturalized American," who has learned to marry Old World knowledge and aesthetics to the New World philosophy that "a man can shape his destiny, if he is willing to pay the price" (192). Because Ventresca believes this "old saying" (192), he is both naturalized and natural, at home, in America.

Ventresca's allegiances to Old and New Worlds, the worlds of peasant and pen; to Italian memory (often cast in less literal terms: longing for familiar food, snatches of dialect, a half-remembered song); to European high culture; to progress and limited assimilation (often in the form of intermarriage as well as education—Ventresca, in fact, reprints a full-page trophy photograph of his Anglo American wife in *Personal Reminiscences*); these allegiances define the complex male selves at the heart of his and so many fine and long-overlooked Italian immigrant narratives.

Chapter 3

Family, Beautiful Women, and "Stupid Ideas about Writing" John Fante's (Italian) Americanness

My great-grandfather's English literacy and his marriage to an American woman made him at least part American. But like the immigrant autobiographers, Peter Patelli was not completely satisfied with assimilation. As he worked to build his company, as the company helped to build the New York subway system, and as Peter grew rich, he continued to search for a more comfortable Americanness, Italian Americanness, unmaking some of the American America had made him.

Like John Fante's father, he laid brick. He built the exterior of his house entirely of brick and mortar, an Italian art, his corner two-story an Italian villa inscribed with his initials, PP. When the house was finished, Peter added, plant by plant, a grape arbor and vegetable garden, putting the finishing touches on his reconstruction of Italy (the finest features of his village), recovering a culture he had seemed to leave behind.

Still, he never entirely retreated from the bustle of American life. Year after year he worked in his American business, read *The New York Times*, vacationed in Cuba with his American business partner, rooted for the Brooklyn Dodgers, watched professional wrestling on television, and spoke to his children and grandchildren in English. (He reserved Italian for cursing lazy or inept employees, especially those who might give Italians a bad name.)

Peter felt the pull of two cultures throughout his life, as he pursued the *impresa* of making himself what he believed to be American, while simultaneously, in grand gestures of *ripresa*, reconnecting to the Italian life he had left behind. Luckily for him, while he was literate and intelligent, my great-grandfather had little time to agonize over his bicultural dilemma, and if he did, he never let on.

John Fante was not so lucky. The often opposite forces of Americanness and Italianness inflicted upon Fante's soul wounds that bled prose alive with exhuberant pain. Fante was born in Denver, Colorado, in April of 1909, the eldest of six children, to an Italian immigrant father and an Italian American mother. Shortly after his birth, the Fante family moved to Boulder, where young John grew up in an environment rife with cultural and familial conflicts. Fante's father, Nick, an immigrant, worked as a bricklayer whenever the Colorado weather permitted. He also played cards, drank, and philandered, squandering his family's rent and grocery money. For this and other reasons, he often fought with Fante's devout mother, Mary, the child of immigrants, who did what she could to shield her children from her husband's tempers. The Fantes sent young John to Catholic schools, where he learned to despise his mother's religion, and where he discovered his three great passions: baseball, women, and writing.

Fante attended the University of Colorado for less than a year before dropping out. In the late 1920s, when Fante's father left the family, Fante moved to Calfornia with his mother and younger siblings. There, he worked in a fish cannery and other hardscrabble places of employ, aspiring all the while to become a professional writer. Fante drew on his experiences during this period for the first of his four Arturo Bandini novels, posthumously published as *The Road to Los Angeles*. In 1932 Fante published his first short story—the first of twenty-eight that would see print during his lifetime—in *The American Mercury*.

Flushed with this early success, he set out on a career as a writer of fiction. Over the next fifty years, however, Fante would publish only six books of fiction. (Since his death in 1983, his wife Joyce has published three more.)[1] We can attribute this meager output to Fante's literary livelihood, screenwriting. From 1934, when he sold his first screenplay to Warner Brothers, through the late 1960s, Fante spent much of his time and energy writing for the screen; yet only eleven of his many scripts actually became films, the most successful of which were *Jeanne Eagles* (1957), *Walk on the Wild Side* (1962), and *The Reluctant Saint* (1962). In the end, Fante's contribution to the Hollywood dream machine and his family's coffers cost him a great deal of serious fiction, and kept him from more fully achieving an important goal, to "cover the true Italian-American scene, as yet pretty much untouched" (Cooney 39).

In the 1970s, Fante developed diabetes and eventually went blind, dictating his final novel, *Dreams from Bunker Hill*, to his wife, who saw to its publication just months before his death. Since then, Fante's work has drawn a fair amount of critical attention, though not nearly as much as it deserves.

In 1995, the State University of California at Long Beach sponsored the First John Fante Conference. A collection of essays that grew from that conference, *John Fante: A Critical Gathering* (1999), as well as conference organizer Stephen Cooper's excellent biography, *Full of Life* (2000), focus on Fante as both an Italian American and a California writer. Although much of Fante's fiction does in fact revolve around Depression-era life in the Los Angeles area, some of his best work, such as the second Bandini novel, *Wait Until Spring, Bandini*, is set in Colorado, his home state.

By Fante's own account, his father worked hard to provide for his family; but as a bricklayer in Colorado—a place one of Nick's fictional counterparts, Svevo Bandini, considers "always frozen, no place for an Italian bricklayer" (Fante, *Wait* 25)—he met with little success. Svevo and Maria, the parents of Fante's fictional alter ego, Arturo Bandini, struggle to make a living and keep their family together in the face of economic difficulty and prejudice. Maria is forced to buy groceries on credit, a necessity that leads her indirectly to discover her husband's infidelity with an Anglo American woman, and leads young Arturo to feel shame that his family's economic failure might be part a result of their Italianness. "He hated Craik [the grocer], that skunk, always asking him if his father was drunk or sober, and what did his father *do* with his money, and how do you Wops live without a cent, and how does it happen that your old man never stays home at night, what's he got—a woman on the side, eating up his money?" (99). Arturo equates economic failure with failure to attain something he often (though not always) craves: an American identity without the qualifier of an ethnic label or the ascription of foreignness.

In *Wait Until Spring,* Arturo's sense of Americanness develops in response to his parents and their situation (Patti 333). "His name was Arturo, but he hated it and wanted to be called John. His last name was Bandini, and he wanted it to be Jones. His mother and father were Italians, but he wanted to be a pitcher for the Chicago Cubs" (Fante, *Wait* 33). At other points in his fictional life, Arturo just as vehemently claims other Italian and Italian American identities. As a fourteen year-old child, for instance, he internalizes his father's ideal Italy as part of his identity, literally crying "for the walls his father had built, the steps, the cornices, the ashpits and the cathedrals, and they were all so very beautiful, for that feeling in him when his father sang of Italy, of an Italian sky, of a Neapolitan bay" (56). At moments like these, it appears that Arturo could not care less to be just plain "American." The young Arturo is forever in the process of developing and redeveloping a love/hate relationship with his fellow "Wops" (Gardaphè, *Italian* 62; Collins, *Fante's* 3). The result of this process is nearly the opposite of Ventresca's pride in his dual identity: a lasting ambivalence toward both his Italianness and his Americanness.

This ambivalence leads Arturo to seek resolution of his ethnic conflict from one source above all others: women. "After his twelfth year the only things that mattered were baseball," and later, in its stead, writing, "and girls, only he called them women. He liked the sound of the word. Women, women, women" (Fante, *Wait* 114). It makes perfect sense that the first "woman" to draw Arturo's attention is the adolescent Rosa Pinelli, an Italian American girl who can represent not just Italianness (Livorni 65),[2] but also Americanness and a possible Italian Americanness. At the movies, Rosa is his means of identifying with twentieth-century America's greatest icons of Americanness, its Hollywood stars. He finds himself "under the spell of that celluloid drug...positive that his own face bore a striking resemblance to that of Robert Powell, and he was equally sure that the face of Gloria Borden bore an amazing resemblance to his wonderful Rosa" (Fante, *Wait* 78). The narrative registers Arturo's delusion that "Gradually Robert Powell lost his identity and became Arturo Bandini and gradually Gloria Borden metamorphosed into Rosa Pinelli" (79). In environments more charged with anti–Italian and nativist sentiment[3]—the streets and parochial (in every sense of the word) schools of the fictional Rocklin, Colorado—Arturo thinks, "Rosa, me and you: a couple of Italians" (118)...I love you, Rosa...he envied her and was proud of her, wondering if those who listened ever considered that he was an Italian too, like Rosa Pinelli" (133).

Arturo's desire to please Rosa conflicts with his poverty. In a misguided attempt to show his love, he steals a piece of jewelry, and presents it to her, an act that leads her to reject him. Rejected, hearing that Rosa has taken sick, Arturo, fearing the permanent loss of Rosa and foreshadowing her death, pleads, "Oh Rosa, please don't die. Be alive when I get there!" (168). In his fantasy, Arturo returns to her triumphantly, from Yankee Stadium, where he is a baseball star and mainstream American hero. "Here I come Rosa, my love," he dreams, "All the way from the Yankee stadium...and here I am at your bedside, just in time, and the doctor says you'll live now, and so I must go away, never to return" (168). Here Arturo is clearly aware of his conflicting desires for American success and Italian American fulfillment, his internalized *impresa/ripresa* conflict, in the shape of a woman. He imagines that he must go "[b]ack to the Yanks, Rosa...The Yanks need me too; but you'll know where I am, Rosa, just read the papers and you'll know. (168) In his ideal world, he will return to Rosa, his Italian American woman, but jet away again, to American adulation.

If he could put aside his quest for American acceptance,[4] Rosa could represent his place in America. "Rosa: tinfoil and chocolate bars, the smell of a new football, goal posts with bunting, a home run with the bases full. I am an Italian too, Rosa. Look, and my eyes are like yours" (116). Unfortunately for Arturo, after Rosa rejects him, she is distanced from him by an Anglo American girl, Gertie Williams, who writes Arturo, "*Rosa told me you made her shiver because you were so terrible. You are a foreigner, so maybe that's the reason*" (242). Then, Rosa dies. In this, she becomes the first of many women in Arturo's life whom he sees as a means of resolving his ethnic conflicts and who, as it turns out, never can.

Fante grapples with such conflicts of ethnicity in most of his early work. In a 1933 letter to H. L. Mencken, Fante wrote of the proposed sociological study of Italian Americans, "'I shall attempt to prove that the Italians in the United States are not only unprincipled murderers but also a stupid gang of lost yokels whose social significance is not in their ability to be good citzens, but bloody clowns: a ludicrous and unsocial people who have forsaken poverty and accepted harlotry'" (qtd. in Collins, "Of Wops" 47). Later in the same letter, Fante backs off his extreme judgment, admitting "his lack of experience with Italians anywhere but in the West, his inability to speak Italian, and the cruel futility of attacking 'the supidities of a few ignorant immigrants'" (47). Although he never wrote the study, Fante did plumb the depths of his obviously conflicted view of his people in *Wait Until Spring,* the only one of the Bandini novels narrated from a third person perspective, as if it were half fiction, half the sociological study of Italian American ethnic conflict he had proposed.

In *Wait Until Spring,* Arturo's conflicts and frustrations parallel those of his father Svevo, who "was a pure Italian, of peasant stock that went back deeply into the generations. Yet he, now that he had citizenship papers, never regarded himself as an Italian. No, he was an American" (74). Still, both Svevo's and Arturo's words reflect uncertainty about their own identities. Like other of Fante's fictional fathers and sons, Arturo and Svevo are frequently obsessed with the term "Wop," alternately deploring it and identifying themselves as Wops, Italian Americans W.ithO.ut P.apers. This obsession is the subject of Fante's 1933 short story published in the *American Mercury*, entitled "The Odyssey of a Wop." Jimmy Toscana, the narrator and protagonist, explains, "From the beginning, I hear my mother use the words Wop and Dago with such vigor as to denote violent distaste" (135). To Jimmy's father, however,

> Wop and Dago are without any distinct meaning, though if one not an Italian slaps them onto him, he's instantly insulted. Christopher Columbus was the greatest Wop who ever lived, says my father. So is Caruso. So is this fellow and that. But his very good friend Peter Ladonna is not only a drunken pig, but a Wop on top of it; and of course all his brothers-in-law are good-for-nothing Wops. (Fante, *Wine* 135)

Use of the term here parallels use of the term "nigger" by some contemporary African Americans and Latinos as a marker of inclusion in a group that finds its identity outside of the social and economic mainstream. To those inside the groups who use them this way, the terms "Wop" and "nigger" are positive or at least neutral markers of identity, although they may be seen as unmitigated slurs by other people of the same ethnic group or people of other ethnic groups. In *Wait Until Spring, Bandini*, Arturo calls himself "the only freckle-faced Wop on earth" (48). Part of him is comfortable or at least accustomed to the label and the not-quite-American identity.

By strict definition, Svevo is not a Wop. He has his citizenship papers, and to him those papers are a declaration of Americanness. But to other characters, Anglo Americans, including the widow Hildegarde, he remains "an Italian" (176), an "ignorant peasant" (198). Svevo is frustrated in his quest for recognition as an American. And to Svevo's greater frustration, Maria, his wife, seems to be "not, after all, an American woman. Nothing about her, neither her complexion, nor her hands, nor her feet; neither the food she ate nor the teeth that chewed it—nothing about her, nothing, gave her kinship with 'the American women'" (74–75). The salt in this ethnic wound is his failure to support his American family by his Italian trade. Svevo takes out his frustration on his wife, on Arturo, and on the other children, verbally abusing them, carousing with Italian *paesani*, and committing adultery with Italian and Anglo American women.

In *Wait Until Spring,* one of Svevo's illicit affairs says more than any other event in the novel about the external American sources of internal ethnic conflict. The Anglo American widow Effie Hidegarde takes a concupiscent interest in Svevo, at least in part because he embodies the forbidden fruit of the lower class, racial/ethnic (married) other. Svevo is subject to the same thrill. When her first attempt to seduce him seems to be falling short of success, she calls him a "fool" and "an ignorant peasant" (198), to which he responds by tearing off her clothes and leaving her "sobbing in her fulfillment" (199).

Their affair comes to a brutal end when the Widow Hildegarde yells at the adolescent Arturo, "You peasants!...You foreigners! You're all alike, you and your dogs and all of you" (265). At which point Svevo defends his son. "Mrs. Hildegarde...That's my boy. You can't talk to him like that. That boy's an American. He is no foreigner" (265) To which the widow responds, "I'm talking to you too!" (265). To which Svevo responds, in Italian, "*Bruta animale!...Puttana!* [whore!]" (265). Svevo's epithet for the widow turns the stereotype of Italian man as brute and sexual predator on its head; the Widow Hildegarde is now the predator, Svevo and Arturo, the prey. More importantly, the outcome of their relationship typifies Fante's protagonists' involvements with Anglo American women.

Fante portrays these involvements as futile attempts to conquer (through sex) a morally vacuous mainstream American society full of women like Effie Hildegarde and Miss Hopkins in *The Road to Los Angeles*. Hopkins is an Anglo American librarian, a "fair white princess" (53), whom Bandini the Italian American, "black and undeserving" (53), can never possess. Arturo's desire for Miss Hopkins stirs his feelings of ethnic, even racial, difference in America, feelings of inadequate Americanness. He admits that a "woman like Miss Hopkins upset me and made me feel absurd" (119). At the moment Arturo as narrator confesses these feelings, Arturo as protagonist transfers his desire for an Anglo woman to a derelict he encounters late one night on a Los Angeles street, who "was a sickly white, like the police photographs of a criminal female. Her eyes were starved and," like Miss Hopkins', "grey and big" (119). Arturo shadows her along several blocks, but when he finally catches up, "something jammed in [his] throat" and he "couldn't even look at her" (124). Unable to approach Anglo America personified in woman, Arturo begins running down the street, fantasizing that he is "the greatest half-miler in the history of the American track and field annals...I was known jokingly among the sport scribes as a 'woman's runner,' because I was so tremendously popular among the feminine fans...Women threw out their arms and begged me to win—for America" (125). This fantasy recalls the younger Arturo's fruitless fantasy of playing for the Yankees and Rosa Pinelli, in *Wait Until Spring*. And in the end, the latter fantasy costs him a chance to connect with the mysterious urchin, another impossible woman. He laments, "You fool! You've lost her. She is gone forever" (126).

It's safe to say that here Arturo the narrator is mocking Arturo the protagonist's fantasy, vanity, and insecurity, but at the heart of that mockery and the insecurity it mocks lies Arturo's burning desire to be recognized by mainstream Anglo America as an American. And while *The Road to Los Angeles*, Fante's first novel, runs from pretentious Bildungsroman to juvenile satire of the romantic Bildungsroman voice, it does occasionally reveal the extent of both Arturo's insecurity and his desire for acceptance. Angry at his own failure to enter the American mainstream, Arturo in his young adulthood calls those who live according to the social norms "sheep! Victims of Comstockery and the American system...Work for this system and lose your soul. No thanks. And what does it profit a man if he gain the whole world and lose his own soul?" (Fante, *Road* 45).[5] Impassioned as they are, Arturo's rants are nothing more than undigested combinations of Nietzche and the communist propaganda so thick in the intellectual air of Depression-Era America.

While Fante makes light of Arturo's anti-establishment denouncements of American materialism and soullessness in *The Road to Los Angeles*, in the more sophisticated *Ask the Dust*, he considers, through the consciousness of a more mature Arturo, the possible conflicts between American materialism and Italian immigrant values. Fante's Italian immigrant characters frequently question American values, condemning American society for its emphasis on money and de-emphasis of family as the focal point of life. Fante left unfinished the manuscript of a novel, "Ah, Poor America!" in which a family of Italian immigrants continually curse America and each other. The immigrant father and son exchange vicious greetings. "'Would that I were forty pounds heavier, three inches taller, and forty years younger! I would surely break your fingers, my beloved son.'...'I am sick'," the son replies, "'The sight of you twists my bowels" (177); while the immigrant mother exclaims, "'Ah, poor America!...Ah, bleeding heart of America, that makes all men dogs!" (Cooney 178). Traditional southern Italian life based on respect, duty, and filial order (Gabmino, *Blood* 1–38) degenerates here in the "filthy American sunshine" (Cooney 178). Italian immigrant grandmother Donna Toscana, in *Wait Until Spring,* bewails the fate of those who become American. "'Ah,

America, thy children shall tear out one another's throats and die like bloodthirsty beasts!'" (91).

Like Donna Toscana, Arturo's parents are, after all, the ghosts of Verga's peasants, folkloric themselves. "He came along, kicking the deep snow...His name was Svevo Bandini, and he lived three blocks down that street. He was cold and there were holes in his shoes" (Fante, *Wait* 11). They are peasants whose lives revolved around the preservation of the family and its members; the preservation of their well-being and honor (Covello 247; Manoukian 20); they carry with them a conception of life as an unchanging cycle (of misery). And while Fante himself never lived as a peasant, he knew the peasant mentality from Ignazio Silone, the Italian author of *Fontamara*, whose work he admired (Wills, qtd. in Cooney 337),[6] and, of course, from his parents.

For Maria Bandini, religion provides a means of personal fulfillment in an alien and hostile American society. The long-suffering Maria, like Oscar Handlin's Uprooted, fixes her "vision on that life eternal which would follow this...If injustice now seemed to triumph, then it was only that retribution should come after" (100). Religion is her escape from an American world in which individuals were often defined by the social status and material wealth she lacks. "And Maria began to climb. Bead for bead, life and living fell away. Hail Mary, Hail Mary. Dream without sleep encompassed her...She was away: she was free; she was no longer Maria, American or Italian, poor or rich...here was the land of all-possessing" (75). Like her peasant woman ancestors, Maria escapes her social and economic disadvantages only through prayer.

Guido Toscana and Svevo Bandini seek similar escape and fulfillment, but seek it through the pursuit of women: either women who represent a pastoral return to Italian youth, like Coletta Drigo, "a flower from the hills of Sorrento" (Fante, *Wine* 96), in the short story "A Wife for Dino Rossi"; or women who represent an Anglo America to be mastered, like the widow Hildegarde in *Wait Until Spring*.

The way that many Italian and Italian American men have rejected strict Catholicism over the last two centuries, Arturo claims to reject religion and belief entirely. He endures the indignities of a Catholic school education and altar boy service, and then reads Nietzche. The result is his declaration, "'I reject the hypothesis of God! Down with the decadence of a fraudulent Christianity! Religion is the opium of the people!'" (Fante, *Road* 23). There is self-parody in Arturo's narration, but also real rejection of his mother's solution. Arturo is more comfortable, but not completely so, with his father's solution. He wants neither to return to Italy, to Italianness embodied in woman, nor to give himself over to Anglo America in feminine form. Yet Arturo's attempted solution to his sense of ethnic alienation is no rebellion against his mother's Old World religion or his father's trans-ethnic romantic adventures. Rejected by Rosa Pinelli, temporarily disgusted by Italian women, he applauds his father's infidelity with the widow Hildegarde. "So give it to her Papa! I'm for you, old boy. Some day I'll be doing it too, I'll be right in there some day with a honey like her..." (Fante, *Wait* 166). Arturo ends up combining both his mother's and father's means of fulfillment in America, by seeking out an American Madonna to worship and defile.

Fante's later fiction presents characters still conflicted, but more comfortable with the pursuit of material success. In *Dreams from Bunker Hill*, the final installment of the Bandini saga, Fante presents an adult Arturo pursuing his American dream of literary/cinematic success and fame. Arturo describes the writing of "Sin City," his first screenplay (which he later disavows). "And away I went: up canyons and down ravines, horse careening, six-guns blazing, Indians falling, blood in the dust, screams of women, the burning buildings, the menace of evil, the triumph of good, the victory of love. Bang bang bang a thrill a minute, the greatest goddam western story ever written" (88). But Arturo derives no satisfaction from his effort, concluding, "It was not a good picture, or an exciting picture, or a mature picture, and as it came to an end and the house lights went on, I saw the weary patrons half asleep in their seats, showing no pleasure at all" (127). The young writer takes cold comfort in having removed his name from the work in time for it not to appear in the closing credits.

In the Hollywood of the 1930s, Fante could not have explored in film, at least not in any serious way, themes of ethnic conflict. Although nativism had been on the wane since passage of the Immigration Act of 1924 (Curran 145; Steele 11), anti-immigrant, anti-Italian sentiment lingered, especially in the West. Louis Adamic, a writer, scholar and Yugoslav immigrant, and a frequent commentator on ethnicity during the period, claimed, "No one of any influence in America today seems to want to raise the old 'welcome'sign" to immigrants" (qtd. in LaGumina 248). In fact, as some still do, xenophobic lawmakers made a habit of blaming all the nation's ills on a great flood of immigration (LaGumina 248)—this in spite of America's net loss of immigrants during the 1930s (Curran 147).

Leading nativist writer Madison Grant, whose *The Passing of the Great Race* and other tracts had both reflected and fostered America's post-World War I nativism, and thus helped win passage of the 1924 Act, published the even more outlandishly racist *The Conquest of a Continent* in 1933, with Charles Scribner's Sons, a major publishing house, placing Italians into the spurious and, by Grant's estimation, "extremely inferior" "Mediterranean" racial category (231). Max Ascoli, an anti-Fascist Italian exile and commentator, who came to the United States in 1931, in his 1940 *Atlantic Monthly* article, "No. 38 Becomes a Citizen," remarks on the persistence of anti-Italian racism in the sort of litmus testing that many African Americans and late-arriving immigrant groups (recently Arab Americans) continue to endure.

> A Wop has to overcome more handicaps than a pure Anglo-Saxon, therefore he has to run twice as fast, or else he will be treated forever as a Wop. An alien, if he wants to have a chance, has to mix in some church or lodge or trade-union, just as, if he knows how to take care of his interests, he has to find his way into some political organization...[I]n order to be fully admitted to the American community one must prove himself to have an American character and bent of mind. Which means, to put it broadly, that this country is made for natural-born Americans, and that Americans are born, not made. (qtd. in LaGumina 254)

For years to come, the "Wop" would remain unfit for the mass movie-going audience, so the vast majority of Fante's screenplays, like Arturo's, focus on the lives, loves and adventures of Anglo Americans, while most of his published fiction (whose audience was smaller and more sophisticated) reflects his desire to "cover the true Italian-American scene" (Cooney 39),[7] to describe Italian American cultural traits and express Italian American views.

In Fante's 1936 story "A Kidnapping in the Family," The narrator, Jimmy Toscana, explains,

> My mother told me of her first meeting with my father. It was in 1910. It was in August of that year, on the feast day of Saint Rocco, the powerful patron saint of all Italians. On that great day the Italians lined the streets of the North Side, and down the middle of the street passed a gaudy parade, with three complete bands and the Sons of Saint Rocco in their red uniforms with white plumes in their hats. The Knights of Columbus were there, and they had a band, and the Sons of Little Italy were there with their band. In fact, everybody who counted was there, including a lot of Americans who didn't count but who came down just to look and laugh, because they thought feast days on the North Side were amusing. (Fante, *Wine* 14)

What Jimmy describes above is a religious procession typical of southern Italian towns, captured in Verga's fiction, and carried to America by the immigrants. He categorizes the procession in American terms, as "gaudy."[8] To show, however, that Jimmy identifies with the Italianness of his parents' world, Fante appropriates the immigrant autobiographers' strategy of holding up an Italian American looking glass to the American observers of Italian American life. Jimmy Toscana's admission that to the residents of an Italian American ghetto other Americans "didn't count" lets readers know that the Italian Americans labeled "inferior" by nativists like Madison Grant and Edward Alsworth Ross might apply the same label to other Americans. Such a reversal suggests Jimmy's positive view of his ethnicity, and would have suggested to readers of the period what might now seem obvious: that Italian American characters (and Italian Americans) are just as complex as other Americans and deserve equal attention.

Jimmy, like Fante's other young men, is himself complex. As often as he expresses ethnic pride, he expresses ethnic self-hatred. In "The Odyssey of a Wop," he confesses, "Thus I begin to loathe my heritage. I avoid Italian boys and girls who try to be friendly. I thank God for my light skin and hair, and I choose my companions by the Anglo-Saxon ring of their names. If a boy's name is Whitney, Brown, or Smythe, then he's my pal; but I'm always a little breathless when I am with him" (137). Jimmy's confession reveals his complexity and allows the (non–Italian American) reader to understand and sympathize with his desire to move from Wop to Max Ascoli's "American character," and perhaps to applaud it—at least for a time. I say for a time, because Jimmy eventually renounces Anglo Americanness with even greater vehemence than Italianness. In the final few paragraphs of "The Odyssey of a Wop," for example, Jimmy meets an Italian American assimilationist and tells readers, "I'd like to paste him. But that won't do any good. There's no sense in hammering your own corpse" (146). The implication is that Jimmy's assimilationist self is dead.[9]

Fante also takes pains to show a variety of Italian American personalities. His characters run the behavioral gamut from *educato*, polite or well-mannered; to *rozzo*, rough or ill-mannered. Witness Dino Rossi and Guido Toscana in "A Wife for Dino Rossi." The *rozzo* Guido in mixed company chides his more financially successful "friend" Dino (one of his wife's former suitors), "'You, with all your money saved, and what has it got you? Nothing! Solitude, loneliness, gray hair, old age...Dino, you must have twenty-five, thirty thousand dollars in the bank, huh, Dino?'" The *educato* Dino responds by lowering his eyes, so that "all of us would suffer with him, for Dino was not a man who boasted of what he possessed; nor was he without generosity, Dino Rossi" (73). Opposite as they are, Guido and Dino are both realistic Italian American male characters.

Often Fante's narratives assume a single character's point-of-view. At moments when the character's situation and feelings are obvious, Fante inserts an Italian word or phrase, usually an imprecation, which reinforces a sense of the character's Italianness and thus suggests that Italianness may play a role in his situation. The best example of this strategy is the narration of Svevo's affair in *Wait Until Spring*, from Svevo's point of view. Svevo's initial impressions of the widow Hildegarde are mixed. He accepts her flattery, but recoils from her Anglo American version of domesticity. "A lunch of lettuce leaves, pineapple and cottage cheese...If Maria had served him such food, he would have thrown it out the window...Tea and cookies. *Diavolo!* He had always identified tea with effeminacy and weakness, and he had no liking for sweets" (180). Here is Svevo's Italianness at work in both consciousness and language. Tea, a symbol of Anglo American culture to a son and grandson of espresso drinkers, challenges his Italianness and manhood, and heightens his sense of difference and conflict over feeling attracted to an Anglo woman, someone alien to his way of life (and certainly to his wife). He falls back, then, on the Italian language, sending all that disgusts him, as well as his own feelings of disgust, to *Il Diavolo*, the devil. Also significant for this reason is his final response to the widow's charging both him and Arturo with foreignness: *"Brutta animale!...Puttana!"* (265). Readers see Americanness through Svevo's eyes, the dehumanizing effect of xenophobia on the xenophobe herself; thus they better understand Svevo's and Arturo's struggle to fit into American society.

Fante employs stock techniques of modernist fiction—hyperbolic psychological realism and the comedy (and tragedy) of the little alienated soul—in his best work, the third Bandini novel, *Ask the Dust.* All of the young Fante's desires, aspirations, and anxieties over (Italian American) ethnicity and male identity, his central themes, take their most powerful form in the 1939 tale, whose roots lie deep in Italian, American, and Italian American experience, and intertwine with the concerns of Italian and American modernist writers.

American modernist writers of the 1920s and 1930s belong to a generation who replaced religion with romantic love (Baskett 94). In T.S. Eliot's "The Wasteland" and other poems, F. Scott Fitzerald's *The Great Gatsby*, and Ernest Hemingway's *The Sun Also Rises,* men rely upon women for a sense of order and meaning to their lives (94). Brett Ashley, Daisy Buchanan, and the various incarnations of Eliot's hyacinth girl grow from the desire to locate fulfillment in feminine form (Viscusi, "Debate" 155), a desire that certainly did not begin with modernism. In the Western tradition, this desire, a quest for divine joy on earth, includes Homer, Lucretius, Dante, and the Italian and Italian American literary tradition of which John Fante is a vital part. It runs from *The Odyssey* through "The Odyssey of a Wop."

In Italian love poetry of the late Middle Ages and early Renaissance, woman was an ideal, to be, in both the secular and religious senses, adored (Symonds 51). The men who loved these women derived "personal force, virtue, elevation, energy" from their "enthusiastic passion" (51). The casting of woman as "ideal being" reaches the classic modernists from the classics via the Provençal troubadours, Cavalcanti, and Dante. *"L'occhi sereni in cui lu lumi eternu"* ("The Peaceful Eyes in Which the Light Eternal"), the work of a minor Sicilian dialect poet, Michele Moraschino, reflects the Italian tendency to equate the love of woman with "the consummation of spiritual felicity, which surpassed all other modes of happiness in its beatitude" (52).

> *L'occhi sereni in cui lu lumi eternu*
> *si dimustra divisu in dui sblenduri,*
> *su', fatali mia dia, s'iu ben discernu,*
> *vivi furnaci di celesti arduri.*
> *Su'stiddi amici a lu chiù forti invernu,*
> *su'chiari aurori a li mei notti oscuri,*
> *su'rai chi imparadìsanu l'infernu,*
> *su'celi serenissimi d'amuri.*
>
> (Spagnoletti and Vivaldi 1207)

> [The Peaceful eyes in which the light eternal
> shows itself divided in two splendors
> are, my fatal goddess, if I understand them well,
> living furnaces of celestial ardors.
> They are stars, friends of the most powerful invernal,
> they are clear aurorae in my obscure night hours,
> they are rays that make paradise of the infernal,
> they are serenest skies of my amours.]
> (translation mine)

Recalling Beatrice, the eyes of woman here are *"rai chi imparadìsanu l'infernu"* ("rays that make paradise of the inferno"), portals to the ultimate fulfillment.

Since the Middle Ages, poets and writers of the Sicilian and Italian diaspora, from Boccaccio to Puzo, have never ceased creating male speakers, narrators, and characters who see women as means of fulfillment. One of these is Arturo Bandini, a narrator/protagonist as alienated (and at the same time comically conscious of his alienation) as Eliot's speakers, Fitzgerald's Jay Gatsby, or Hemingway's Jake Barnes. Arturo acts and thinks like Jake Barnes, except that Arturo, an American by birth, though the child of an immigrant, remains throughout his fictional life within the geographical confines of the United States. These geographical confines are also the tragicomic confines of the American-in-the-making, the subject of assimilation, not expatriation. Still, in spite of circumstantial differences, Arturo's story resembles Jake's. Each is the story of a man trying to lead a comfortable, comforting, familiar, fulfilling life in a world of uncertain values. Each attempt is a mighty struggle.

Fante may indeed have had Jake Barnes in mind while writing *Ask the Dust*. In his 1941 article about Fante for *Common Ground,* Ross Wills makes clear that Hemingway was on a short list of American contemporaries Fante admired. "[Fante] frankly looks up to Steinbeck, Hemingway, and James T. Farrell, although he has no doubt that when he has as many books behind him as they, he will have equal recognition" (Cooney 337). In *The Road to Los Angeles*, Arturo tells Jim the Bartender that when it comes to writing, "'I'm like Hemingway. I always do it second-nature" (Fante, *Road* 118). If Fante did pattern the Arturo Bandini of *Ask the Dust* after Jake Barnes, he took into account both the strengths and weaknesses of Hemingway's protagonist.

In spite of his demoralizing experience, Jake maintains a semblance of what we may call traditional American and Christian values of industry and sacrifice, particularly sacrifice for his fellow disillusioned expatriates, especially Brett Ashley. Jake's challenge is to rely upon those values to see him through the isolation and humiliation of his post-war, expatriate existence" (Reynolds 61). Arturo too faces a test of values. His test, however, occurs in America, his "native" society, but one whose values he never fully internalizes. Nineteen-Thirties Los Angeles is to Arturo as much a moral desert as 1920s Paris is to Jake a moral wasteland.

Arturo, like Jake, faces his test in a hotel, a shelter but not a home. Living "in the very middle of Los Angeles," a city proverbially built of men's dreams, Arturo upbraids himself, "You dream and you wish, but you go on through the wasteland" (97). The wasteland Arturo sees is one not only of "restless dust," which sullies everyone and everything around him, but also one of hollow men and women. Arturo describes them as

> The old folk from Indiana and Iowa and Illinois, from Boston and Kansas City and Des Moines, they sold their homes and their stores, and they came here by train and by automobile to the land of sunshine, to die in the sun, with just enough money to live until the sun killed them, tore themselves out by the roots in their last days, deserted the smug prosperity of Kansas City and Chicago and Peoria to find a place in the sun. And when they got here they found that other and greater thieves had already taken possession, that even the sun belonged to the others...[they were] doomed to die in the sun, a few dollars in the bank, enough to subscribe to *The Los Angeles Times*, enough to keep alive the illusion that this was paradise, that their little papier-mâché homes were castles. The uprooted ones, the empty sad folks, the old and the young folks, the folks from back home. (45)

Arturo sees, like the apparition of faces in a crowd, "Faces with the blood drained away, tight faces, worried, lost. Faces like flowers torn from their roots and stuffed into a pretty vase, the colors draining fast" (161). This is the "brutal wilderness" (164) of modern life as Fante imagines it, the condition of a society in which religion has lost its ability to provide order and meaning. In place of real hope for fulfillment, Fante's Los Angeles holds out to Arturo the illusion of hope. Its amoral, desert climate fosters in him a false sense of self-importance.

Although Arturo's disillusionment and sense of rootlessness spring from the same alienation and homelessness that Jake Barnes experiences, from some of the same sources that feed what Fante's fiction casts as the misery of west–streaming Anglo Americans—"Smith and Parker and Jones" (Fante, *Ask* 46)—these feelings also spring from the Italian dimension of Arturo's psyche. And herein lies the Italian American difference of Fante's brand of modernism. Arturo explains, "It was Smith and Parker and Jones who hurt me with their hideous names, called me Wop and Dago and Greaser" (46). Like other Italian Americans and other ethnic Americans of the last two centuries (including the Mexican Americans and Filipino Americans Arturo himself calls "Greasers"), Arturo is made to feel ashamed of his ethnicity. His shame and resentment emerge as the narrative of *Ask the Dust* progresses. He feels compelled to pronounce himself, as his father does in *Wait*

Until Spring, "an American, and goddamn proud of it" (44), although he goes on to rail against Americans'anti-Italian American prejudice, as in the above passage. As he struggles to resolve the conflicts of his Italian Americanness, he maintains an attachment to his heritage and his people. Studying the box scores of baseball games, he notes "with satisfaction that Joe DiMaggio was still a credit to the Italian people" (11), and admires other Italians, Casanova and Cellini (90). Arturo plays to American prejudices here, by identifying with Casanova and Cellini, both of whose memoirs helped create the stereotype of the hot-blooded (yet cold-blooded), sexually predatory Italian man. At the same time, he expresses pride in his Italianness, by praising DiMaggio, the quintessential 1930s and '40s symbol of Italian success in America (Moore 171).

Still, Arturo lives doubly alienated. Even the American keeper of the hotel in which he is a paying lodger frowns upon his Italian name, while his Italian family remains at a geographical and emotional distance. To console himself, he is reduced to writing his mother of his troubles and waiting for inadequate written responses. Longing for home, he thinks,

> If someone only loved me, even a bug, even a mouse, but that too belonged to the past...I thought of home, of spaghetti swimming in rich tomato sauce, smothered in Parmesan cheese, of Mamma's lemon pies, of lamb roasts and hot bread, and I was so miserable that I deliberately sank my fingernails into the flesh of my arm until a spot of blood appeared...I was God's most miserable creature, forced even to torturing myself. Surely upon this earth no grief was greater than mine. (28)

The lost Italian American soul pines for the comforts of family, in this case the culinary comforts—spaghetti, tomato sauce—easily identifiable as Italian by Fante's American readership. As in *Wait Until Spring* and *The Road to Los Angeles*, Arturo tries to construct an idealized Italian family life, which, for him at least, never exists. At the same time, he internalizes twentieth-century American images of Italians as spaghetti benders, in an attempt to Americanize his view of the world.

As Arturo lacks the comfort of his mother's food, his *Weltanschauung* lacks the comforting presence of a divine Madonna, of religion, which he also misses, admitting, "Myself, I am an atheist" (22)..."all the gods have deserted me, and like Huysman [sic] I stand alone, my fists clenched, tears in my eyes" (27). Like Des Esseintes, the anti-hero of Huysmans' novel *Á rebours (Against Nature)*, Arturo wants to believe, but as "God's worst enemy" (Fante, *Road* 158), when he "said a prayer"..."it was dust in my mouth"

(Fante, *Ask* 99). To make matters worse, Arturo also perceives, again like Des Esseinte, that the world—in his case the Anglo American world—is itself on if not over the brink of moral bankruptcy. It is the world of Nathanael West's *Day of the Locust*, full of bitter Todd Hacketts, wretched Homer Simpsons, and idolized Faye Greeners; a vulgar world of materialistic, unbelieving masqueraders from whom "Perhaps Christ heard. If He did, He gave no signs" (West 129); a world akin to the spiritual and moral vacuum inhabited by Jake Barnes and Brett Ashley (Holman 139). Arturo's values alone, like Jake's, fail to sustain him. He needs a way into an America he can live with, a viable center of his universe. Unlike Huysmans' novel, which examines the consolation of art, and very much like *The Sun Also Rises, Ask the Dust* explores the possibility of woman as a modern man's way into society, as his center.

As Brett is Jake's symbol of hope for a better life, Camilla Lopez is Arturo's. Inspired by Fante's romance with artist's model Marie Baray, Camilla is Arturo's non-Anglo, non-Italian woman idol. By having Arturo tenaciously pursue Camilla, Fante commingles modernist deification of women in fiction with Italian and Italian American Madonna worship. Italian and Italian American men have always demonstrated "in their devotion to the Madonna a faithfulness to the women they had left behind" (Orsi, "The Religious" 323). Devotion to the Madonna is also an idealization of woman, present as well as absent. Into the mix, Fante adds a distinctly Italian American sense of optimism and possibility, the sort of optimism that carried so many Italians, like Fante's father and my great-grandfather, overseas (Green 24). This optimism, though oft-disappointed, permeates Arturo's narration. "Los Angeles, give me some of you!" he exclaims, "Los Angeles come to me the way I came to you, my feet over your streets, you pretty town I loved you so much, you sad flower in the sand, you pretty town" (Fante, *Ask* 13).

Arturo's persistence in pursuit of Camilla (the saddest of all flowers in the L.A. sand), if not always hopeful, creates at least the illusion of hope, a persistent illusion shattered only at narrative's end. The pursuit of illusion has always been a quintessentially Italian art form. In his landmark sociological study, *The Italians,* Luigi Barzini makes a strong case that in Italian culture "transparent deceptions are constantly employed to give a man the most precious of all Italian sensations, that of being a unique specimen of humanity" (Barzini 79). Arturo's illusion of optimism is likewise a form of deception, delusion; it is his attempt to persuade himself and Fante's audience that he is a classical hero by virtue of possessing the object of his desire and imaginings, Camilla Lopez.

For Arturo, Camilla is "a Mayan Princess and [The Columbia buffet]"—Columbia, after the Italian, Christopher Columbus, was, of course, the pre–Anglo name for America—"was her castle" (Fante, *Ask* 41). Over her objections, Arturo calls her "Little Mexican princess" (61). For him, she embodies the New World in its pristine state, before it fell subject to the corruption of Spanish conquistadors and then the racism of Anglo Americans. For him, California itself is "Camilla's land, Camilla's home, the sea and the desert, the beautiful earth, the immense sky, and far to the north, the moon, still there from the night before" (159). But Arturo's visions of Camilla and her land are simply that: visions, projections of his own long-standing desires.[10] Through their relationship Arturo attempts to rewrite the entire cultural history of North America.

Even before meeting Camilla, Arturo wants to possess a "Mayan princess." "Oh for a Mexican girl!" he fantasizes, "I used to think of her all the time, my Mexican girl. I didn't have one, but the streets were full of them...Aztec princesses and Mayan princesses" (15). Given Arturo's tendency to escape reality through fantasy, his desire to idealize Camilla comes as no surprise. What does come as a surprise is his success in doing so. By embracing Camilla, Arturo learns "to embrace his own status as an alien and outsider" (Collins, "Of Wops" 48). In this sense, embracing Camilla equates to transcending American cultural history. Arturo pursues not only Camilla, but also one of the many "strategies of cultural identification (Bhabha 292) open to ethnic Americans alienated from Anglo American society.

Many Depression-era Americans regarded Mexican Americans—typically swarthier than Italian Americans and in a better geographic and political position to immigrate to America—with even greater suspicion than they did Italian Americans. In a 1930 article for the *Saturday Evening Post*, entitled "The Mexican Invasion," Roy Garis urged further restriction on immigration and labeled Mexicans in particular as undesirables, "men of few wants, apathetic, without ambition, not concerned with the future" (Simon 89). In many quarters, Mexicans remained anathema to an American society accustomed to notions of Nordic superiority—as expressed in Grant's *Conquest of a Continent* and Kenneth Roberts' "The Existence of an Emergency" in *The Saturday Evening Post* (Simon 88). Arturo is an Italian American, not quite low man on the American ethnic totem pole—as he makes clear by his slurs of Camilla—but still a racial and cultural other in his society. In order to feel less alienated, more like the majority Anglo Americans, he, like other Italian Americans in the 1930s (and after), adopts a mainstream attitude of bigotry toward dark-skinned minorities. So he both loves and disparages Camilla for what, not who, she is. At the same time, in trying to connect with a Mayan princess, Arturo strives for unity with the land before it became an America that makes him feel his Italian difference. He looks to absolute racial otherness in an Anglo world, to American Indianness, as an alternative to assimilation. He seeks, in short, to alleviate his feelings of alienation from American society, to resolve the conflict between his Italian identity and American identity, through Camilla.

Although she turns out to be too worldly for her own and his good, Arturo persists in the belief that Camilla is "so charming, so innocent" (Fante, *Ask* 61). He repeats this bit of self-delusion with the far more jaded and literally scarred Vera Rivken, insisting that she too, a Jewish woman from the East Coast, who bears a strange wound, a wound symbolic of ethnic prejudice, between her legs, is a "Mayan princess" (94). As his lips kiss the surrogate Vera, his mind conjures Camilla.

> "Open your long fingers and give me back my tired soul! Kiss me with your mouth because I hunger for the bread of a Mexican hill. Breathe the fragrance of lost cities into fevered nostrils, and let me die here, my hand upon the soft contour of your throat, so like the whiteness of some half-forgotten southern shore. Take the longing in these restless eyes and feed it to lonely swallows cruising an Autumn cornfield, because I love you Camilla, and your name is sacred like that of some brave princess who died with a smile for a love that was never returned." (130–31)

Arturo fancies Camilla in absentia more than a vision of pristine Columbia; he fancies her a "sacred," Madonna-like conduit to "a half-forgotten southern shore" (130), a reminder of Italian roots and of an earlier, kinder American society of his dreams. He also imagines her a victim of European exploitation, of a "love that was never returned," which he fears he himself may not return. As he embraces Vera/Camilla, Arturo announces, "I'm a conquerer...I'm like Cortez, only I'm an Italian" (94). In this last comment we see Arturo's attempt to believe in the Anglo American myth of a "masculine destiny": a version of manifest destiny in which the "American" man—an identity, remember, that Arturo desperately wants to claim—makes the New World his own by displaying prowess "in the Southwest not only on the battlefield but also in bed" (Takaki 176).

Yet Arturo, impotent when he has the chance to take Camilla, can never completely identify with American masculinity. He thus treats Camilla also as a touchstone for his own otherness. Though several times he anguishes over his *Italianità*, at other times—alone and with his Mayan princess—he affirms it by refusing to identify with Anglo traits. When Camilla remarks on his freckles, stereotypically Nordic specks of physiognomy, Arturo replies, "They don't mean anything" (42). He seeks an alternative identity, holds on to his *Italianità*, which, while it is not necessarily palpable, links him with DiMaggio, Cellini, and *La Madonna Santa*.

After committing the "mortal sin" (96) of imaginary adultery against Vera, Arturo exhibits discomfort with Nordic rationality as an antidote to what Grant, Ross, and other American racial theorists of the early twentieth century might have called his Mediterranean passion.[11] "This is bad, Arturo. You have read Nietzsche, you have read Voltaire, you should know better. But reasoning wouldn't help. I could reason myself out of it, but that was not my blood. It was my blood that kept me alive, it was my blood pouring through me, telling me it was wrong...let it carry me swimming back to the deep sea of my beginnings" (96). This sort of blood imagery recurs in *Ask the Dust* and is associated with *Italianità*. Anglo Americans and those under the influence of Anglo American culture appear to Arturo to have "faces with the blood drained away" (161). Their passions and morality are pale, attenuated. Arturo, on the other hand, feels the blood of Italian tradition, as well as passion for an ideal America, coursing through his veins.

Arturo's belief in blood countervails his obsession with rational thought, particularly with Nietzsche. *Beyond Good and Evil* is the subtext for *The Road to Los Angeles* and most of Arturo's interactions with women. Section 232 of *Beyond Good and Evil* resonates most clearly.

> [Woman] does not want truth: what is truth to a woman! From the very first nothing has been more alien, repugnant, inimical to woman than truth—her great art is the lie, her supreme concern is appearance and beauty. Let us confess it, we men: it is precisely *this* art and *this* instinct in woman which we love and honour: we who have a hard time and for our refreshment like to associate with creatures under whose hands, glances and tender follies our seriousness, our gravity and profundity appear to us almost as folly...We men want woman to cease compromising herself through enlightenment: just as it was man's care and consideration for woman which led the Church to decree: *mulier tacean in ecclesia!* (164).

Arturo's Nietzchean attitudes mark both him and Fante as mysogynists, but more importantly, they reinforce the notion that he seeks to possess women, as powerful social, ethnic, and sexual fetishes.

After considering the tragedy of "Smith and Parker and Jones," Arturo sends Camilla a telepathic apology, and expresses the difference they both share.

> I have vomited at [Anglo American] newspapers, read their literature, observed their customs, eaten their food, desired their women, gaped at their art. But I am poor, and my name ends with a soft vowel, and they hate me and my father, and my father's father, and they would have my blood and put me down, but they are old now, dying in the sun and in the hot dust of the road, and I am young and full of hope and love for my country and my times, and when I say Greaser to you it is not my heart that speaks, but the quivering of an old wound, and I am ashamed of the terrible thing I have done. (47)

As Arturo understands it, his and Camilla's compatibility stems from an essential otherness, the "wound" of prejudice they (and Vera Rivkin) constantly suffer in Anglo America. Arturo perceives this essential connection in Camilla's voice, which "talked to my blood and bones" (114). The two would-be lovers share a sense that America is made up mainly of a "they" to be daily confronted.

Arturo grows ever more staunch in the belief that he should protect both Camilla and himself from corruption by forming a family with her. "I love you Camilla I want to marry you," his telegram reads (71). She tears it up, but each time she rejects him for Sammy, her Anglo lover, Arturo, instead of giving up, steels his resolve, until, in a final futile attempt to reestablish family life, he carries Camilla wasted and broken to a new house on the Pacific shore. Arturo's interior monologue makes plain that Camilla might signify family and not just romantic passion—though he certainly seeks the latter in her. "We didn't have to be married," he insists, "brother and sister was alright with me. We could go swimming and take long walks along the Balboa shore" (156). More than anything, what Arturo seeks on the shore belonging to Camilla, to Balboa, to the American Indian tribes, and *not*, in his opinion, to Anglo America, is companionship, support, the understanding of a familiar.

When Camilla and Arturo finally do try to make a home together, Camilla is unable to perform wifely duties as Arturo would define them. Instead of cooking and cleaning and staying home, she smokes marijuana and, from time to time, runs away. Arturo's Italian American upbringing has taught him to believe that the woman of the house should manage domestic affairs.[12] Finally, he recognizes that Camilla has already lost connection to in both Latin tradition and American society. He comes to believe that in modern Los Angeles, she is a "captured child" living inside a "curtained trap," "a creature without spirit or will" (151, 148, 138); or, as Fante calls her in a 1938 letter to his cousin, Jo Campiglia, "a beautiful Mexican girl who somehow didn't fit into modern life" (Cooney 152). Like Jake Barnes, Arturo, at where it concerns Camilla, is sexually impotent, unable to free his idealized woman, powerless to save her, his potential family, from the degradation of modern life. Camilla is too indigenous to the land, the dust, for Arturo to possess her as his own symbol both of perfect assimilation into an ideal America and imperfect ethnic identity. He is, in the end, on his own.

In *The Sun Also Rises*, Jake's impotence symbolizes the failure of his (and his society's) values. The same is true of Arturo in *Ask the Dust*. His Italian American values can neither keep him from suffering the effects of prejudice, not can they save the woman who is his only hope for redemption. Modernism's influence on Italian American writing is startling here. Consider that the sexual manifestation of moral failure, a man's physical incapacity to have sex with a woman, is rare in Italian and Italian American literature—a literature whose male protagonists often feel compelled to lay claim to the right woman, regardless of circumstance (Dante), and often to marry outside of the Italian tribe (Puzo's Michael Corleone) (Viscusi, "Debate" 157–65). Even Arturo's father, who fails morally and economically in America, succeeds sexually with the Widow Hildegarde.[13]

Nevertheless, in *Ask the Dust,* Arturo finds himself unable to lay sexual claim to Camilla. He confesses, "I drew my hands over her belly and legs, felt my own desire, searched foolishly for my passion, strained for it while she waited, rolled and tore my hair and begged for it, but there was none, there was none at all...no lust, only fear of her, and shame and humiliation" (Fante, *Ask* 68). Alone later, Arturo fashions himself a comical Jake Barnes.

> All that day it was on my mind. I remembered her brown nakedness and her kiss, the flavor of her mouth as it came cold from the sea, and I saw myself white and virginal, pulling in the pudgy line of my stomach, standing in the sand and holding my hands over my loins. I walked up and down the room. Late in the afternoon I was exhausted and the sight of myself in the mirror was unbearable. (70)

Jake Barnes, who admits,

> Undressing, I looked at myself in the mirror and the big armoire beside the bed...Of all the ways to be wounded. I suppose it was funny...My head started to work. The old grievance...Probably I never would have had any trouble if I hadn't run into

> Brett when they shipped me to England...[T]he Catholic Church had an awfully good way of handling all that. Good advice, anyway. Not to think about it...Then I couldn't keep away from it, and I started to think about Brett and all the rest of it went away. I was thinking about Brett and my mind stopped jumping around and started to go in sort of smooth waves. Then all of a sudden I started to cry. (Hemingway 30–31)

If he were not pursuing a woman, Jake would have no trouble. But he must pursue Brett, perceiving in her a life force, a center. A similar imperative, "the delight to know that I could possess her" (Fante, *Ask* 124), drives Arturo. Sadly for him, as for Jake, circumstances do not allow.

Both Arturo Bandini and Jake Barnes are impotent, because both are victims of their idealized woman's corruption and their own. Jake is a victim of World War I, its physical toll and disillusioning outcome; Arturo is a victim of the American Dream of equality and success, its economic and social disappointments resulting from cut-throat competition and prejudice. Jake's corruption is obvious: a war wound rendering him incapable of making woman and family the moral center of his universe. Arturo's corruption is less so: a mysterious inner ache brought on by Fante's projection of the American Dream, one which de-emphasizes morality, while emphasizing individual achievement and material success at any cost. In this sense, Arturo represents a lost generation of Italian Americans, namely all those Italian Americans—immigrants, first, second, or third generation citizens—who identified themselves as Italian American, at a time, between the World Wars, when America had no place for such a category.

Although he worries about Camilla and the idea of family, Arturo spends more time and words worrying about the success of his literary career, about individual fame and prestige. He acknowledges that "I had come [to California]," away from family and traditions, away from his Italian half, "with no purpose save to be a mere writer, to get money, to make a name for myself and all that piffle" (123). For him, as for Jake, writing provides the only path to glory: a path which, Fante intimates, is a poor substitute for the satisfaction of family and (com)passion. In this context, writing becomes "piffle," nonsense, the practice of meaninglessness, the absence of fulfillment.

At the very moment Arturo finds himself unable to possess Camilla, he retreats to his editor "Hackmuth's letter and thoughts that remained to be written" (68). Arturo links writing with spiritual sterility and moral as well as literal death, through the character Sammy, to whom Camilla remains tragically devoted. Sammy's name, cool posturing, and romantic notions of the

Wild West symbolize Uncle Sam. He spends his dying days writing bad westerns he hopes will sell, rather than embracing Camilla—whom he refers to, in a letter to Arturo, as "the Little Spick" (121). Through Arturo's account of Sammy, Fante criticizes the American substitution of profit for love as the artist's inspiration: a poor motive that corrupts Arturo (and Fante) too,[14] robbing him of his (com)passion.

If *Ask the Dust* presents a hierarchy of degraded romantic nobility, Arturo is its king. He may belittle Camilla, he may not love her for herself, but at least he loves and respects her as someone "deeper rooted than I" (123), as a symbol of some lost, ideal America, an alternative to his conflicted Italian American identity. Camilla occupies a lower station in the hierarchy, because she loves Sammy out of denial of her ethnicity. She insists, "I'm *not* a Mexican!...I'm an American" (61). Denying her Mexicanness, she covets Sammy, who, she believes, personifies Americanness. Sammy, the least noble of the trio, only wants Camilla in order to live out his male Anglo American fantasy of dominion, sexual and social, over the (Indian, foreign, dark-skinned, female) other. He advises Arturo, "Mexican women...don't like to be treated like human beings. If you're nice to them, they walk all over you" (121).

The corrupt realm he shares with Sammy and Camilla forces Arturo to delude himself about the pursuit of his ideal woman, his ideal life in America. When Camilla asks Arturo, "Why are you so mean?" he replies, "There is not the slightest drop of enmity in my system. After all, you can't be mean and still be a great writer" (115, 116). By this point in the narrative, Arturo's actions have entirely contradicted his claim to bard's grace. He has already damaged or threatened to damage Camilla, Sammy, Vera, and a host of neighbors. Certainly, Arturo never calls another character "friend," and although he wants and needs her, his corruption and selfishness render him "not good for Camilla Lopez" (128). Camilla provides Arturo only fleeting "beauty like the love of some dead girl" (97). Even before she disappears, Camilla dies as Arturo's Beatrice, she all along as wounded as he, as Jake, as Brett. In the end, Camilla's death is also "the failure of a dream," Arturo's dream of a comfortable and viable ethnic American life.

Chapter 4

Electric Blue Italian: Anthony Valerio and the Rewiring of Italian American Male Identity

One evening over dinner, I asked Anthony Valerio how he had developed his distinctive narrative style—a tragicomic, free associative prose current. He answered that he couldn't help it, when he sat down to write, he had an idea of the way his narrative would go, but after a while, that idea gave way to what he called the flow, the "electricity" of his brain. It is this electricity that charges Valerio's fiction with exquisite wisdom and humor, and makes it an essential literary representation of contemporary Italian American consciousness. Valerio's fiction acts as a nexus of narrative circuits connecting his characters' consciousness to the consciousness of other important Italians and Italian Americans, connecting the characters and Valerio's audience to the eternal sources of Italian American culture and identity. These circuits glow blue with characters' sadness at their initial distance from the past and from their Italian (American) heritage.

Valerio was born on May 13, 1940 to two Italian American Bensonhurst natives, William and Gertrude Valerio, both of whom figure prominently in his work. He passed his childhood in Bensonhurst, a then exclusively Italian American section of Brooklyn, rebuilt by and for immigrants like my great-grandfather and first generation Italian Americans, who used their post-war American wealth to surround themselves with the comforts of Italian cafés, Italian bakeries, Italian groceries, Italianate two-family brick houses, and hand-painted shrines to the Madonna, Saint Anthony, and other half-Catholic, half-pagan icons of the *Mezzogiorno*.

William Valerio earned a good living as a beloved resident dentist, and so Anthony enjoyed a comfortable upbringing among a sea of relatives and colorful Italian American personalities. A natural comedian, the younger Valerio was expelled from several secondary schools. As punishment for his antics, Valerio's parents forbade him from playing ball in the street (Gardaphè, *Dagoes* 219). Luckily, sitting on the sidelines taught Valerio to bear witness to the Italian American scene in Bensonhurst (Valerio, Personal). The future author did eventually graduate high school and enroll at Columbia College, from which he received his Bachelor of Arts in French literature in 1962. During his college years, he discovered writers such as Gogol and Proust, who would become his first literary influences (Valerio, Personal).

After college, in part to escape a looming military draft, Valerio attended medical school in Italy. He left for Bologna in the autumn of 1962, and spent some of the next three years studying medicine, but more time writing and wandering through Italy and Spain. While living in Barcelona, Valerio began to think of himself as a writer (Valerio, Personal); and from the beginning of his literary life took an interest in Italian and Italian American cultural history as a subject for fiction. One of his first efforts is a story—written, Bohemian style, on Japanese rice paper, in red typewriter ink—about Mussolini and his mistress, Clara Patacci, and the events leading up to their hanging (Valerio, Personal).

Filled with romantic notions of the writer's life, he returned to America in 1965 and began a literary career. In 1967, he entered the publishing industry and within a few years had become a successful editor, freelancing for firms such as McGraw-Hill and Grove Press, all the while cultivating an original narrative voice—sometimes waking up at three a.m. to write before work (Valerio, Interview, "Italian"). In 1972, Valerio left publishing to teach creative writing, which he has done intermittently for the past twenty-five years. Since the early 1980s, he has devoted most of his time to writing.

Although he claims, "I had no desire to publish at that point," Valerio's short story, "The Skyjacker," appeared in 1977, in George Plimpton's *Paris Review*. Based loosely on a brief news item in *The New York Times,* it is a story told from the perspective of an Italian American soldier, imprisoned for hijacking a commercial flight from California and forcing the pilot to land in Rome. It begins,

> To get a circumcision in Italy is a major operation. For example, if you are born in the General Clinic in Bologna, the gynecologist will not do it. You have to go to Florence. The Italians are a type who if they cannot find what they are looking for in one store they go no further, especially if it means they will not die. I plan to tell the Italians about themselves. (80–81)

Valerio wrote the story in order to find out, he half-jokingly claims, "what the soldier was thinking" (Valerio, Personal), but it is certainly the beginning of a literary life devoted to telling "the Italians about themselves." The soldier's return to Italy, it turns out, is an important precursor to the comic, nostalgic, pastoral elements in Valerio's later fiction; an early indicator of his characters' Italian American hard-wiring.

The narrative current of the story flows from simple thoughts to extended cogitations. In this case, a mundane conversation with a visitor sets the narrator along a winding cultural course.

> He speaks a broken-down English and Italian. I am supposed to understand. As far as this is concerned, the Americans and the Italians are on equal footing. I did not understand much of the English in Seattle. My father always spoke of Italy in Italian-American and I assumed that what I didn't know about the language amounted to what I didn't know about the country itself. Michelangelo and Mussolini are dead. No language barrier. David, from what I've seen of him in pictures, is not of a mind to say much, and Mussolini's son is a piano player. Leonardo is alive though. He is floating in the Tiber face down. He is disgusted. America had no Leonardo five hundred years ago. Cochise wasn't even born then, nor was Spiro Agnew. Yet Alitalia has fewer planes than TWA. Leonardo is my friend or else he would not have given me his plane. (81)

Valerio suggests that this particular narrator's wiring may be wound a bit too tight, but the flow of his thoughts does reflect a recognizable, normal confusion: the confusion of the hyphenated American who has lost a great deal of his original culture, most notably its language, in the process of Americanization, struggling to reconstruct it. This is where the story of Valerio's life as a writer of Italian American narrative begins, and where the story of my great-grandfather's life ends. Throughout the 1960s and 1970s, Peter Patelli watched as his friends' children and grandchildren, and even his friends themselves, the ones still alive, left a close, concrete Bensonhurst of neighbors' open doors, front porch conversations, and walks to relatives' houses and Sunday *mangioni*, big dinners, for the lawn and two-car comfort/isolation of suburbia. He worked, but for someone else now—his own company and American success story a piece of the past. He drove home from work past the Italian American cafés, bakeries, and groceries, past the buzzing artifice of their red, white, and green neon signs advertising *Italianità* (not yet understood as *Italo-americanità*) to suburban exiles and American tourists. He dreamt now of not only his memorial Italy, but also the old American face of its memory. That face, in its changes, grew both less and more familiar with time.

As he drove along, Peter thanked America for a prosperous life, and was glad to have taught his children and grandchildren to do the same. He had also taught them to remember their Italianness as much as their Americanness, instructing by example, by traditional habit. He dreamt of another time, but took comfort in the signs that the spirit of the Bensonhurst that he—like Jack Cusimano, Valerio's fictional "master builder of Bensonhurst" (Valerio, *Valentino* 47)—had helped construct, lived on, not only in its streets and two–family brick villas, but in the minds of its Italian American descendants.

The narrators of Valerio's books live disconnected from the sources of their ethnicity by ambition, and simultaneously alienated from mainstream American society by their cultural memory. Valerio makes their contemporary lives one terminal point of his narrative, which he links, often humorously, often poignantly, to the sources of Italian American culture and identity, to the real and mythological lives of other Italian Americans past, present, and future.[1]

"Having a lot of trouble" with his girlfriend (Valerio, *Valentino* 16), Anthony, the synonymous and romantically challenged narrator of Valerio's second book of fiction, *Valentino and the Great Italians*, transmits his sad reflections to a great Italian American personality and source of Italian American male identity, Frank Sinatra; he hopes for a surge of enlightenment in return. "On this forty-sixth celebration of my name day, St. Anthony of Padua, I would like to send Frank Sinatra my condolences. Now I am able to commiserate with him when on entering his forty-sixth year he sought to settle down with a good woman too. His friends were married: there was a Mrs. Martin, a Mrs. Bishop, a Mrs. Davis and a Mrs. Lawford" (18). Commiseration allows Anthony to examine Sinatra's dilemma for possible solutions to his own; to connect with a useable Italian American past.

The narrative collapse of time involved and the reference to Saint Anthony allow for the narrator's simultaneous connection to other great Italians.

> A name day is a day of truth. Just as on their daughters' wedding days all Dons grant any wish whatever, on their name day they are obliged to tell the truth. The truth is that St. Anthony was not born in Padua, he performed his miracles there. He was born in Portugal. As an infant he was sickly and was transported with care to Africa. He gained strength and on the way back to Portugal stopped off in Padua and stayed.
>
> The truth: is it possible for one man, even an Italian one, to romance the likes of the following women, with prime time taken out for a marriage to his first and eternal love, his Italian sweetheart: Lana Turner, Jill St. John, princess Soraya, Ava Gardner…?
>
> A name day is also a festive one, but the truth is I've been alone all day with

> northerly gales blowing pollen in through my window. My door is kept open a body's width by a dagger. (19)

Although Anthony's contemplation of dons as great Italians does prefigure the use of don as truth-teller in his third book, *Lefty and the Button Men* (originally published as *Conversation with Johnny*), I do not mean to suggest, nor does Valerio, I think, that "all Dons" are great Italians in the manner of Saint Anthony. In the narrator's search for truths, stereotypes, and ironies, the don is just a single associative point along the circuit of Italian American culture. Inside of a few paragraphs, Anthony wires his life to the lives of Frank Sinatra, St. Anthony of Padua, Garibaldi (by the allusion to Garibaldi's use of dagger as doorstop), and unnamed mafiosi—drawing from them, he hopes, the power to solve his problems and achieve a fulfilling Italian American identity.

Valerio's most powerful associative search of this sort is 1986's *Valentino.* The book grew from a brief piece entitled "The Great Lover," which appears in the author's 1982 collection, *The Mediterranean Runs Through Brooklyn.* After reading *The Mediterranean*, an editor at Freundlich Publishers requested more portraits of great Italians and Italian Americans. Eventually, Valerio would complete and publish twenty-two of the portraits in a single volume. In a televised interview, Valerio called the book "a document rather than something that fits a genre," "a weave between history and personal history" (Valerio, Interview, "Italian")—the personal history not of Valerio himself, but of Anthony the narrator as representative Italian American man wired to Italian and Italian American history.

When Guernica Press reissued *Valentino* in 1994, Peter Carravetta, to date one of the few serious commentators on Valerio's writing, called the book "writing that makes you think of an autobiography, creative journalism, or semiserious *scherzi* [jokes or tricks] worthy of the highest journal tradition, pictures drawn through words, frames of life...Or a book about the social imaginary of a binational, bicultural group, melding History with Fantasy" (Carravetta, "Valentino" 348–49). This weaving of history and personal history with fantasy harnesses the current of Italian American culture as seen through the narrator's life and the lives of significant Italian (American) personalities. This brand of narrative hybridism resembles that of the Italian American autobiographies discussed earlier, insofar as Valerio's narrator tells his story as protagonist with disdain for the protagonist's (and other characters') desire to escape the Italian elements of their Italian Americanness. The narrator, Anthony, advocates the *ripresa* of Italian and Italian American narrator, Anthony, advocates the *ripresa* of Italian and Italian American culture as a remedy to his own American *impresa* as protagonist. Anthony acts on his impulse to reclaim but not be imprisoned by his Italian heritage, by activating the narrative circuit that joins his history with those of his cultural forbears.

Anthony's impulse arises from his dissatisfaction with the process and product of Americanization, symbolized by movement away from the Italian American pastoral homeland, Bensonhurst. In a portrait of his male cousins, "The DiGeorgio Boys," Anthony imagines the personal life of a cousin who has forsaken the old neighborhood, his ambition to follow in his father's footsteps, and his family, for a life apart.

> Instead of looking back to Bensonhurst for a new way, he goes to a college up in Buffalo. Here his voice deepens, his genitals flourish, he discovers psychology. In the laboratory one day the aspiring psychologist next to him, a girl...They go outside and knee-deep in snow Bobby Boy says, "You Italian?"
>
> "No," says the girl. "A problem?"
>
> "No. I've been through enough upheavals without insisting on a cultural link."
>
> "Well, thanks a lot," the girl says, affronted.
>
> "There I was," he goes on, "about to be an engineer, we move to Connecticut, my father gets fired, and now I'm up to my ass in snow, surrounded by nervous laboratory animals."
>
> "I love you, Bobby."
>
> "You do?"
>
> "Yep. You know, we could make a life together concentrating on the abnormal personality."
>
> "Think so?"
>
> "Yes, I do."
>
> They hug and kiss...He commits himself to the girl and in the privacy of his mind decides to exercise [sic] the DiGeorgio spirit amid the mountains, fresh air and psychotics of upstate New York. (Valerio, *Valentino* 199–200)

Anthony's disapproving tone comes through loud and clear: Bobby Boy is wrong for exorcising the DiGeorgio spirit and, he implies, psychotic as well for giving himself over to America outside the Italian American circuit of acquaintance and custom. He, Anthony, knows better than to disconnect himself from Italian America.

At the same time, Anthony is wary of becoming trapped in the Italian American circuit of tradition. In the portrait entitled "Enrico Caruso," he considers the case of Uncle Mike,

> the first doctor in Bensonhurst to convince Italian cardiacs that they might have to leave Bensonhurst a while in order to go to the Mayo Clinic in a place called Min-

> nesota for what was called a bypass. Mike himself traveled alone to Texas to witness experiments on a dog's heart. Mike DiGeorgio was also the first doctor in Bensonhurst to convince Italian cardiacs that they had to spend a little time in a hospital—it wasn't a disgrace, their families could come." (219–20)

Mike is a cross-cultural pioneer, discovering and naming practices foreign to his community. Eventually, Mike's forays and non-traditional practices and manners earn him a bad reputation in Bensonhurst. He marries a non-Italian and accumulates "a stock portfolio worth millions" (224). Anthony describes his ostensible transgressions in a communal voice. "Only the Syrians in Bay Ridge accumulated that kind of portfolio—was he keeping information from his landsmen? He had bought into a loan company—was he squeezing debtors? After Don Salvatore died, Mike became Head of the Family, and we cared about his reputation. His reputation was also ours" (224).

The community's concern for Mike's unorthodox upward mobility derives from centuries old *Mezzogiorno* peasant values, values born of traditional economic deprivation, suspicion of the nobility, and perilous attempts to advance one's status. In life, as in Valerio's fiction, these values have survived several Italians American generations. Instead of making spectacular investments in the stock market, Italian Ameircans have, until recently, tended to make reliable investments in home, property, and family business (Gambino, *Blood* 131). The operative communal desire here, and the one with which Mike must contend, is a lingering wish for security in closed Italian circuits, those Italian American enclaves that preserve old country wisdom, custom, and preconceptions (Mangione and Morreale 129).[2] In this sense, the Italian Americans of these enclaves, the residents of Valerio's Bensonhurst, carry on the legacy of Verga's peasants.

The community's sentiments speak, as they do in Verga, with a single narrative voice. Don Salvatore, recognizing that his son is ready to marry and settle down, says to him, "'It's sad, Mike, and a tragedy when you think that Caruso's wife didn't know how to make spaghetti either! So marry an Italian girl, *figlio mio*, and live in Brooklyn—otherwise, what will you eat?" (220). Food here, treated as the stuff of life, symbolizes *Italianità* resistant to all manner of geographic, political, economic, and social change. Other powerful fetishes of *Italianità* in Valerio's fiction include the "mushroom noses," shared by the majority of Italian and Italian American characters in all three of his books, joining them as the people of a single Diaspora.

Mike's reaction to Don Salvatore is typical of Italian American characters caught between their strivings for American economic and social success, and their continual recourse to Italian and Italian American culture. Mike must weigh his desire to remain within the Italian American circuit against his desire to move up in the larger society. There is no guarantee that either society will fully accept him. The same is true for many characters and real Italians Americans in similar situations prior to the 1970s, when anti-Italian prejudice was stronger (Alba 75). Mike resolves his dilemma by remaining in Bensonhurst, but secretly wanting his and his wife's mutual "love to congeal into an impenetrable barrier against the Italians in the neighborhood, his insulated family" (Valerio, *Valentino* 222). His answer to communal objections to his lifestyle is

> Who cares! What was I supposed to be? A bricklayer with dignity? A mafioso with the reputation of being a good family man? A smiling, sweet-talking barber who doubles as a bookie? A longshoreman who drives his kids crazy because he wants them to become professional men? A housepainter who plays a good game of pinochle? I became a doctor, a good doctor, and if they want to call me a prick, let them! At least I'm a consistent prick! (225)

In rehearsing a litany of Italian American male stereotypes, Mike nullifies them; in him, Valerio's narrative electricity brings the Italian American professional man to life in American fiction.

Valerio, who himself has chosen a profession far less common among Italian American men than doctor, presents male characters who desire to live both within and beyond the circuit that is Bensonhurst. Their dichotomous desire takes a dichotomous narrative form, a rendition of the Italian American social imaginary as concurrently pastoral and mock pastoral. Valerio's narrative implies the modern choice between "economic [career] advantage" on one side and "other" (pastoral, spiritual, social, cultural, non-economic) "ideas of value" (Williams 61), here the values of Bensonhurst, on the other. For this reason, Valerio's narrator lives in self-imposed "exile in Manhattan," sad "that there are no more Christmas Eves in Brooklyn" (Valerio, *Valentino* 211), that the Italian American traditions he associates with his family and with a long lost Bensonhurst of the 1940s and 1950s are unavailable to him. As much as *Valentino* is a celebration and narrative connection to Italian and Italian American cultural icons, and a celebration of the Italian Diaspora beyond the New World village of Bensonhurst, it is Valerio's reconstruction of Bensonhurst as Italian American pastoral. It is a place to which his narrators repeatedly attach the epithet "God's country"

(221); a place, like the native villages of the immigrant autobiographers, in which the inhabitants may commune with transcendent cultural forces (Boelhower, *Immigrant* 103); a place and time inhabited by God-like figures such as the ancient Pietro LaClacca, Anthony's boyhood neighbor.

The adult Anthony describes LaClacca from the point of view of "little Anthony boy," out for a bike ride around his tree-lined block.

> He would be working in his garden, stooped low among his flowers and ivy, and he emerged from it like a beast from the forest, slowly, with measured steps. He was big...He had hair white as snow and a square, red face...
>
> "Hi there, little Anthony boy!"
>
> It was a great booming voice. It shook the trees and froze the boy. He dropped his hands from the wheel, tensed his arms and surrendered his neck. The old man pinched a section of skin and pulled up. The boy rose to his tiptoes and raised his head as high as it would go. He looked at the tops of the trees. Gritting his teeth, he said, "Hi, Mr. LaClacca.
>
> The old man didn't let go. He squeezed harder and said it again: "Hi there, little Anthony boy!"
>
> The boy's mind fought for the magical words that would release the grip. (Valerio, *Valentino* 113)

The narrative not only casts LaClacca as a folkloric giant, but also as an immigrant, a direct link to Old World language and customs, a conduit to the pastoral Italian village, a connection to "a closed but dynamic folkloric environment" (Boelhower, *Immigrant* 106), a source of the cultural current that feeds Anthony's identity.

> [Little Anthony boy] might also understand that his old neighbor with the white hair and eager face was lonely, his heart was in the country of his native language, and that in America he had used his hands instead of his mouth. The vise-like grip of the neck, the pain, was a way of saying that he *understood* English and was waiting to hear something meaningful, something other than hello or goodbye. Something about the work he had done with his hands maybe. Yes, that was it—he was waiting for a compliment on his cement work. Fixed in the cement that bordered his garden and the iron fence that separated his house from his neighbors were thousands of semiprecious stones. (Valerio, *Valentino* 113–14)

Notable in this passage, first of all, is the Italianate cement work—still as much a feature of Bensonhurst masonry as the masonry of Southern Italian villages, a detail that links hemispheres, centuries, and cultures. Also notable is the shift to LaClacca's point of view. Suddenly, in a supreme act of "ethnic semiosis" (Boelhower, *Through* 86–87),[3] Valerio enables little Anthony boy (and grown–up Anthony as Narrator) to transcend time and space, by splicing an old Italian immigrant's consciousness with his. Suddenly, little Anthony boy can read the mute flourishes of ancient Italian "genius" (114) in their signal modern American form, from the creator's vantage.

Assuming that pastoral myths are, when they are creations of individual consciousness, private pastoral myths (Marinelli 5), we can easily identify the source of Valerio's pastoral. One central private myth appears in *Valentino*, and recurs throughout Valerio's fiction: the narrator's epic infantile tears.

> [F]or the first five years I cried. Night and day I cried, sometimes eighteen hours at a stretch, and the day I was administered morphine, I cried twenty hours...I stopped crying for longer periods outside than in, and so every mid-afternoon, my mother wheeled me away from the El, I cried, but if she wheeled me toward New Utrecht Avenue, I stopped crying even when my carriage was still. A train passed every ten minutes or so, twenty-four hours a day...[M]y mother turned the carriage around and tilted it so that I could see the train in the full glory of its roar and speed, the tracks tremoring, sparks shooting down into the shadows. I goo-gooed and drooled and tried to sit up. A serious look came over my face as my eyes followed each window, each car. When the last one sped by, I was now looking at the immense azure sky and fell back and listened to the train slow down as it pulled into the Seventy-ninth Street station. (238–39)

Adult Anthony links infant Anthony's tears to the movement of trains: a real electric and preternatural force connecting the pastoral Italian American homeland of Bensonhurst to the world beyond. "[M]y mother burrowed the carriage through the snow and stopped in the middle of the street to show me the train from directly underneath...She allowed the sparks to rain down on us, they diffused before reaching us, but for a few seconds up there it was like a spray of Stardust" (240). From the time he is a baby, Anthony is magically connected to Bensonhurst, to its aura (the sparks), but uncomfortable there. Throughout his life and the lives of Valerio's other narrators, psychic connection to the pastoral homeland remains at once comfort and discomfort.

In *Lefty and the Button Men*, the narrator, Nicholas, responds to his Don/confessor's wish to know "the whys and wherefores of your fuckin' tears" (62). Nicholas continues Valerio's lachrymose macrotext, tearfully explaining to the Don, Johnny, how the powerful memories of Bensonhurst's affections assuage his sense of alienation, yet how those same memories never fail to turn him blue with sadness.

> The women shopping in the shadows of el, they waited for me. In front of Termini's bread store, Arturo's photography studio, Mrs. Palermo's grocery store.

They gathered around the carriage, and my mother proudly stepped aside. These women looked down at me, smiling, tears flowing. They said that in their entire lifetime they had never seen such long curly lashes..."We will never again see such beautiful eyes, such beautiful lashes."

"And you did!" Johnny exults, his voice cracking. "You stopped crying and blinked and blinked your eyes for them! Your screams cleared the way for a lifelong image, a pair of beautiful eyes shining in the center of a hard life." (63)

As Valerio's narrators often do, Nicholas uses the quaint phrase "the shadows of the el" to mark the boundaries of his Bensonhurst and to suggest the feeling of security he derives from recalling it. The women of Bensonhurst, the life blood of the entirely Italian American world of Termini's, Arturo's, and Mrs. Palermo's, adore the baby Anthony. The memory of their communal love continues to sooth him (and them) throughout his narrative life; it becomes a part of his identity. When, as an adult, he boards the Manhattan-bound train, Anthony remains connected to Bensonhurst and his part in its life, as if by the electric current coursing through the rails beneath him.

From book to book, Valerio sheds ever brighter light on a personal history that dramatizes the qualities, virtues, and deeds of those who populate his Bensonhurst pastoral. His characters include the narrators' friends, family, and most significantly, his dead father. In *Lefty*, Nicholas describes his father's sacrificing, out of a sense of duty to Nicholas's mother, the love of his life. In *The Mediterranean Runs Through Brooklyn*, the narrator extols his father's physical beauty as a young man. In *Valentino,* Anthony celebrates his dying father's memory of that beauty.

[P]erhaps my father would recall his own physical beauty, of which he was so proud. Women in their seventies stop me on the street and say, "Are you Edward's son? You look just like him."

"Yes," I answer with pride.

"Your father was so handsome." (Valerio, *Valentino* 117)

Moving from a description of his father's beauty, Anthony recalls the time of his mythic ugliness, his cancer-riddled body. "My father was grotesque now. Only I could look at him. His grotesqueness compounded my love. I adored him. Exactly half of his head was bald and half had some prickles of gray hair." (118). Both images of Edward here are significant because larger-than-life. His life and death become first actual, then memorial force, pulling Anthony—although he is no longer subject to the geographical and social limitations of Brooklyn—back to a folkloric Bensonhurst life of pure qualities, ugliness and beauty.

Anthony conjoins the beauty and tragedy of his father's life with that of the eponymous lover Rudolph Valentino. He speculates that as a child his father may have gone to see Valentino's *The Four Horsemen*; and when further along he identifies the aged Edward as an Indian, he again identifies him with Valentino, by announcing in the next sentence, without any transition, "One of Valentino's guides was an American Indian named Black Feather" (118). This narrative flow, independent of syntactic connection, distinguishes Valerio's work.[4]

Anthony explains,

> It does not matter where Valentino was born, he is immortal, exists in the air everywhere, but when he was walking the earth he felt that he had left a part of himself in his homeland...Italy...a part as real as an arm or a leg to which he joined himself whenever he returned home. It was a warm, intimate, secure feeling that he could not capture except at his birthplace and its vicinity, a feeling so strong that it displaced disappointments and expectations and elevated the commonplace to wonders of the world. (143–44)

Of course, both Edward and Anthony himself are infused with Valentino's spirit, the feeling of belonging to an ideal homeland, an idyllic Italy or Italian America. In recognizing that "[b]etween Valentino and his father was a psychic connection the way there is between lovers and birds flying in a flock" (150), Anthony recognizes his own connection to his Italian American father; to their common "loneliness so desperate that it threatened his existence and could only be assuaged by a woman, a kind word from her, a caress" (151). This mythical woman is the memory of the women who adored baby Anthony; and she is the women whom Anthony and other of Valerio's characters, in the way of Arturo Bandini, seek out as means of fulfillment.

Time and again in the narrative, Valerio connects a Bensonhurst character like Edward to a mythical Italian American personality, pushing the boundaries of Bensonhurst, enlarging the Italian American circuit to infinite circumference. This connection of Bensonhurst history with Italian (American) myth operates also on the level of language. Anthony imagines a conversation between Valentino and the townspeople of Valentino's hometown. When the pragmatic villagers tell the emigrant movie star they would like to buy his dead parents' house because they could use the land, Valentino's response takes the poetic tone of an Italian folktale.

> "What are you talking about?...First of all, from wherever I am I will come back when it snows to clear a path for the passing carriages. With my massive

> shovel I will remove the snow from the winding path leading to the front door. I will come back for the garden, to trim the hedges and water the honeysuckle and snowballs, and I will clean the windows so that the sunlight will continue to shine in. I will come back just to sit in the chairs, move among the rooms where we ate, laughed and worked." (147–48)

Valentino's honeysuckle and snowballs appear also in Anthony's own parents' garden, a comfort to his dying father. The presence of the flowers suggests that Anthony, animated by Valentino's own electronically projected spirit, or transferring his own desires to the Italian American legend, will never give up his connection to Bensonhurst, the homeland of his people. Of course, the villagers' reply to Valentino hints at the difficulty of maintaining that connection once one has left: "Why, that little prick!" they exclaim, "he needs a kick in the ass!" (148). Their vulgarity translates the coarseness of the Italian peasant into Brooklynese, drawing Old World Italian *cafoni,* unrefined peasants, and New World *paesans*, "landsmen," into one continuous circuit of ethnicity.

The tone of the above exchange typifies the comic tone of Valerio's narrative in general, which are, then both pastoral of an Italian American homeland and, in equal measure, mock pastoral: that is, pastoral lit by a narrative consciousness aware of the limitation and irony of pastoral memory. This Proustian brand of memory transcends time and heals the scars it leaves (Stead 297). Valerio's narrators, after all, live in self–imposed exile from Bensonhurst, the circuit they idealize and could tap into again—through closer contact with other family members and childhood friends but choose not to. They would like to comfort themselves by reentering the Italian American circuit, reprising the culture of their origin, but at the same time they would like to remain outside, to escape its cultural biases and join a larger American (and global) community.

When Anthony's Argentine lover charges him with homophobia, he responds by blaming the community whose cultural forces have shaped him, and by mocking its values.

> "You have to understand...that where I come from, Bensonhurst, Brooklyn, there was no such thing as a homosexual. Nobody lived alone or with just another man or woman. The houses were too big, two- and three-story brick and shingle. Married couples lived in them and they had kids, the kids I played with in the street. Each member of the couple had known each other since they were kids. The prospective brides hung around while the boys played ball in the lots." (Valerio, *Valentino* 182)

Anthony's affection for Bensonhurst remains, but so does his desire to move beyond its circuit of traditional Italian American (vaguely Catholic) values; so when he calls Bensonhurst "God's country," he does so with more than a hint of irony.

Anthony's desire to transcend Bensonhurst leads him to include many historical citizens of the world among his "Great Italians": Christopher Columbus, the Mona Lisa, Giuseppe and Anita Garibaldi, and Enrico Caruso, for example. Among these, Giuseppe Garibaldi occupies a central symbolic place. He is a champion of Italian unity, an early Italian American (After his years in Brazil, Garibaldi lived for several years on Staten Island, sharing a house with the inventor Antonio Meucci), a bi-hemispheric Italian crusader for liberty, and a global Italian cultural icon. Valerio has repeatedly turned to Garibaldi's story as object for admiration and aspiration. And judging from Valerio's work on the subject, Garibaldi is as important for being Anita Garibaldi's husband as he is for being a model of generosity and courage. In *Valentino*, he recreates their life together as epic love story. At their first meeting, Giuseppe tells Anita, "*Tu devi esser mia*" ["You must be mine"] (81). And, tragically, as she is dying of fever, he tells the attendant physician, "You can not imagine...all that his woman has Done for me, and how tenderly I love her" (170). The story of Garibaldi becomes then, for Valerio, the story of a bygone love, like the love Valerio's narrators remember receiving from the women of Bensonhurst, and like the love they long for from their impossible mates. (Valerio's most recently book is, in fact, a biography of Anita.)

The stories Anthony tells of Garibaldi connect him to the hero's generosity of spirit, vision, and practice of universal brother and sisterhood. On a "visit with" the statue of Garibaldi in Washington Square Park, Anthony reflects on the great Italian's early life.

> During his lifetime he saved sixteen people from drowning. When he was eight years old he saw a woman washing her clothes in a deep, wide ditch. She fell in, pinioning her head beneath the pool. Encumbered by his game pouch, the boy nevertheless lifted her head gently and eased her over onto his lap. During his first days in Rio de Janeiro, where he had exiled himself following an abortive attempt to rouse to revolution the Royal fleet in Genoa, Garibaldi saved a Negro slave from drowning. As the youthful exile walked past the three-story white granite houses, he heard the crackling of whips and cries of pain. In Rio de Janeiro of 1832 slaves were not allowed to wear shoes or ride in the mule-drawn buses, and when they died their bodies were tossed into a pit. While strolling along the waterfront he saw a slave fall into the sea. Garibaldi saved him. The slave was a giant of a man, Santos was his name; and with boiling eyes he said to Garibaldi, "I wish to join you..." (79).

Anthony's Garibaldi moves freely between Italy, South America, and New York, achieving communion as easily with an African slave, an Argentine farm girl (Anita), the inventor of the telephone (Meucci), and anyone he finds in need, as well as with the people of his native land. In short, he transcends his original community, tapping into a global circuit—as Anthony and Mike DiGeorgio attempt to do.

Valerio sees himself as having been "set off on a journey [by my original community]...I take with me all the nurturing, positive and negative" (Valerio, Interview, "Italian"). One effect of this nurturing is Valerio's sensitivity to prejudices and stereotypes. Carravetta believes that Valerio's tales depend for their interest upon

> the way he spins out prejudices on commonplaces and with a light hand unknot [sic] them in a variety of settings and situations, leaving us to savor the disturbing possibility that these stereotypes may indeed be, if not pre-determining the fate of certain encounters, then probably co-determining the unfolding of the semantics, disclosing newer understanding. (Carravetta, Review 351)

These "prejudices on commonplaces" include American prejudices toward Italian American men; lingering stereotypes of Italian American men as criminal brutes and/or sexual predators.

A dozen years ago, John Gotti made the cover of *Time* magazine. Meanwhile, in films like *Jungle Fever* and *Do the Right Thing*, Spike Lee was exploiting the preconception of an Italian American male tendency toward violence and sexism (Viscusi, qtd. in Verdicchio 187). (Unfortunately, Lee, a gifted filmmaker, continued this exploitation in 1999's *Summer of Sam.*) Around the same time, the cast of Saturday Night Live was running a series of sketches in which a pair of lecherous waiters with Italian accents smother female patrons of their restaurant (usually guest hosts of the show) with unwanted amorous attention, calling them *"Bellissima!"* until they succeed at forcing them into sexually compromising positions. And then, of course, there has been Mario Puzo, whose *The Godfather*, in its filmed version, has infiltrated the canon of American film and the consciousness of the nation. Not to mention his best–selling 1996 novel and 1997 hit Mafia miniseries *The Last Don,* which "captivated over fifty-two million viewers," according to network promos for its 1998 sequel, *The Last Don II.* Even in death, Puzo continues to peddle the Mob, in his 2000 novel, *Omertà.*

In 1999, the criminal brute stereotype (and to a degree the Latin lover stereotype) took new shape, thanks in large measure to Martin Scorsese's 1990 film *Goodfellas*, which presents a realistic, humorous portrait of Italian American gangsters. This recent mafia comedy, typified by *The Sopranos* and *Analyze This*, has embellished Scorsese's wise guys, making Italian American criminals appear ever more vulnerable—especially in their need for the comforts of Italian American food, language and women, as well as psychoanalysis.[5] In spite of its partial debunking of the criminal brute stereotype, even this recent wave has left intact the gangsters' ruthlessness in illicit pursuit of sexual satisfaction and money. None of the directors of these comedies (Martin Scorsese, David Chase, Ivan Reitman), therefore, recasts the image of Italian American men through the gangster stereotype as thoroughly as Valerio does in *Lefty*. Valerio charges *Lefty* with satiric energy, transforming current stereotypes of Italian American men, by making those stereotypes the subject of a mock-Socratic dialogue between two such men: Johnny, the Italian American don, and Nicholas, the Italian American artist—also the narrator—who identifies himself as a lover, with the qualification, "By lover I don't necessarily mean a big man with the ladies, I mean the way I view everything" (Valerio, *Conversation* 128). Nicholas is a successful writer who has left the Brooklyn source of his Italian American identity for a life in Manhattan and parts beyond, an artist in search of beauty. According to Valerio, Nicholas is also, regarding his links to Italian American culture and society, "at the end of the line. Not only is he allergic to wheat" and therefore pasta—a symbol of cultural sustenance in the book and in Italian America generally—"he's also having an affair with a Jewish young lady" (Valerio, Interview with Lopate), Lefty, a woman much more a part of the American establishment than Fante's Vera Rivken. To make matters worse, he lives in Greenwich Village, a world away from Bensonhurst. One day, Nicholas, lonely and alienated from both the society in which he lives and the society from which he comes, decides to return to the old neighborhood for a psychoanalytic sit–down. He asks the don, "Now I want the truth—what went wrong, Johnny, what went wrong with me?" (Valerio, *Conversation* 16). This is a supplicant meeting of the kind Puzo made famous, except that here the don is more cultural therapist/confessor than benefactor or powerbroker. *Analyze This* and *The Sopranos* feature dons acting not as therapists, but as patients, themselves in need of cultural therapy. Only in Valerio's work does a genuine Italian American consciousness hold the key to fulfillment. This dynamic is one way Valerio succeeds in his attempt to "humanize the don" (Valerio, Interview with Lopate), to destroy the stereotype, by having him sit and listen as Nicholas begs him, "Help me to change, Johnny. Help me to change from a lover to an ordinary man" (128)

During their first session, Nicholas tells Johnny that he has returned on a whim of essential connection. "'I saw your eyes on the cover of *The New York Times Magazine*...I knew they could see into everything, even into my subconscious, and they cleansed it of its penchant for debunking my own, for creating the beautiful lie. Rather than the stereotype, I opted for the beautiful lie" (16). But the "beautiful lie" Nicholas has opted for is, at least at first blush, another Italian American male stereotype. He has eschewed the role of don and chosen instead that of Latin lover.[6]

> Instead of becoming a doctor or a businessman, I became a lover. I, a Brooklyn boy, born the same year as you, at the outset of the war, from a good family, father a doctor, half-Sicilian, half-Neapolitan, the Sicilian predominant in that it was handed down by my mother. Every day for the past nine years I sat alone with my notebooks and gave love away to strangers. No Puccini, no family, no *paisani*—alone and silent. My desk looked out toward the Hudson River, and on the sill was a white scalloped bowl replenished each day with fresh water for the sparrows...After bestowing the daily gift, I was still alone in a ramshackle pre-war building a block away from Christopher Street when I love women, Johnny, love them as much as my distant children and dead mother. (16–17)

Beginning their fictional lives as two apparent stereotypes, Nicholas and Johnny prove to be novel Italian American male characters: the cultivated, vulnerable lover and the compassionate don.

Throughout the narrative, Nicholas plays Socrates to Johnny's Glaucon, responding to the latter's unreported questions with digressions on his life as lover, writer, Italian American. In appropriating a classical model of reason, Valerio counters the myth of Italian hot-bloodedness (Scapp 37). In response to Johnny's quiet prompts, Nicholas employs reason to parse the emotion, passion, and action of his and Johnny's experience as Italian American men.

He begins by reading the stereotypes of Italian American men that *The Godfather* (which Nicholas mentions several times in the book) perpetuates. The first of these is the sexual predator, embodied in Sonny Corleone, who is "so generously endowed by nature that his martyred wife feared the marriage bed as unbelievers had once feared the rack" (Puzo 15). The folkloric language of Puzo's description presents Sonny literally as a larger-than-life figure. It also reveals that like most of the women characters in Puzo's novel,

Sandra Corleone suffers for a Corleone man: in this case, for Sonny's sexual satisfaction. Lucy Mancini, the lover whom Sonny shoots through with the "savage arrows of his lightning-like thrusts; innumerable; torturing" (28), likewise suffers; she suffers indignity in her relations with physically normal men, for her generous genital endowment, the same sort of endowment that makes Sonny legend. The only sexual consolation for her abnormally large genitalia is Sonny's abnormally large genitalia, which she loses, along with Sonny, when he is gunned down. In this sense, like Sonny's wife, she is sexual prey.

Valerio recalibrates this relationship in *Lefty*. Nicholas, the lover, instead of preying upon his woman, is preyed upon by her. Lefty uses Nicholas as an orgasm machine, and tortures him with talk of marriage, though she herself is married and never commits to divorce. "[I]f you marry me," she teases, "you'll have to make love to me every night. Every single night" (Valerio, *Conversation* 26). While admitting he would marry her, Nicholas struggles to keep up with her sexual demands. During their interview, he confesses to Johnny that after one sexual encounter with Lefty, he found himself "totally spent, ricotta through and through" (22). Here Valerio begins the exposition of Nicholas's vulnerability, which he fully reveals in a chapter entitled "The Paramour." "After I revealed my symptoms to the doctor," Nicholas explains, "I was prepared to drop my pants so that he could examine my muscle, determine whether it had the capability any longer of filling with bone. I was prepared to stimulate myself behind a curtain" (42). Nicholas learns from the doctor that his problem is psychosomatic. The treatment: a virility pill, which Nicholas comically Hellenicizes. "Xanax, the Sicilian champion come to fight for the Greeks, steps out from the ranks, and with a booming voice heard all around the countryside calls out the Trojan champion..."Stressimpotence! Stressimpotence! Let's you and me settle this dispute with hand-to-hand combat. Winner take all!" (43). Nicholas wins the battle but loses the war. Lefty ends their affair, calling him after the breakup to ask if she can include in her novel a death scene of their relationship, a scene that he has conjured. By making Nicholas Lefty's literary as well as sexual victim, Valerio does not so much explode, as he transposes a stereotype. The Italian American man may be the seduced as well as the seducer.

Valerio transforms the stereotype of Italian American man as brute through similar means. Lefty uses Nicholas for literary inspiration and, especially, for sex, responding to the Italian "animal" she sees in him. Valerio pushes this ethnic exoticism *ad absurdum*. Instead of having his characters refute Italian animalism—an artless strategy of protest—he allows them to acknowledge a grain of truth in the stereotype, while at the same time exploding it. "Let's face it, Johnny—all of us, we *are animals*...There's Jake the Bull, Sly the Stallion. Each and every one of us is a fox. But the winds may be changing. Stallone has a script on his desk about the life of Giacomo Puccini" (Valerio, *Conversation* 66).

Nicholas himself admits to being a chimp, nearly as intelligent as Lefty, but not as cunning in desire. Over the phone she wheedles, 'Your prick is beautiful. I think of it every night before I go to sleep.'" (68). Later, Lefty "instructed, 'Make me wet.'...The chimp's hands, fingers, lips, tongue—all worked up a prodigious lather. Lefty bolted from the yellow club chair, eyes darting wildly. 'Get in bed. I must have you inside me.'" (68). Nicholas may be the chimp, but it is Lefty who acts from animal desire, not love. Thus, Nicholas is neither seducer nor brute, though it is possible that the culturally assimilated American woman in whom he seeks fulfillment may be both.

Johnny represents the most popular brute stereotype of Italian American men, the criminal brute. According to the criminal brute stereotype, Johnny, as a Mafia don, should whack those who refuse the offers they can't refuse. Valerio takes the expectation of such violence and obliterates it with a jolt of absurdity. Michael Corleone sends his lieutenant and even his own brother out for rides from which they never return. In the chapter "Lesson on Paradise Island," Nicholas suggests that Johnny take a similar ride with an Italian American "kid professor," whose father was murdered, who disrespects his wife, who invents a gangster past, and who generally does his best to live up to stereotypes of Italian American men.

> So what do you say, Johnny? Let's take this kid aside and talk to him, put the arm on him a little bit. Let's you and me and couple of the boys take him away for a weekend from the environs of his dark memories and his misrepresented wife. We'll fly down to Paradise Island, and over cocktails on our veranda overlooking the palm trees and emerald ocean, you place your arm gently around the kid's shoulders, muss up his hair a little like he's a boy again, and softly, your compassionate eyes staring into his frightened ones, you say, "We understand about your father, that the image of his bullet-riddled body is all-powerful, that you feel profound pity and filial love and well-founded hatred and bitterness and shame—but all this can dwell inside side by side. Keep them the fuck that way. And your wife, it looks funny how you're talking about her. She's loyal and hard-working, supportive and, from all reports, beautiful. You secretly love her, don't you? See...It's alright to proclaim your love for her to the world. Finally, remember, always remember, that you're a professor now and not a thief. For the time being, we have to tolerate our crime and our

> culture, but your job is to promote the culture, not the crime." Here, Johnny, I suggest you make a wide sweep of your free arm, taking in all of us and the trees and the ocean, and your face suddenly goes dead and you say in your most ominous, sweet tone: "Do this for me. Do this for Johnny, at least until the likes of us are gone. OK...? Good. Now let's all go to the jai alai games." (*Conversation* 53–54)

Johnny will take a little ride to rehabilitate, not brutalize his quarry, his fellow Italian American. As Nicholas imagines the scene, Johnny's voice will sound not ominous, deadly, but "ominous, sweet," in that order. He will not teach a stereotypically Italian lesson by making an example of his victim, but will teach his fellow Italian American a lesson by unmaking an American stereotype. He speaks against macho gangster posturing; for emotional honesty and balance; against hot-headed, hot-blooded exploitation and abuse.

Later in the novel, Valerio uses the current of absurdity to animate Don Pippo, a surreal composite of Nicholas and Johnny, and a symbol of the imperative to emphasize Italian American culture over Italian American crime. Suggesting the power of artistry and cultural awareness to transform identity (of The Don, The Artist, and all Italian Americans), the aged Don Pippo begins his narrative life as a character in one of Nicholas's short stories. He takes both Johnny's and Nicholas's place (literally inhabiting Nicholas's apartment). He then dies, freeing Nicholas's soul from feelings of shame associated with his attachment to the old neighborhood, from the pain of lost love, and from his cosmic loneliness (Hack 4). Finally, Nicholas is free of the conflict between his attachment to the Italian American community and his desire to share his love outside of that circuit; free now to be both a citizen of Italian America and a citizen of the world.

Don Pippo, in announcing his own demise, sets a vision that Nicholas and other Italian Americans might follow.

> I am Pippo Napoli-Sicilia and I am the last of the great Dons, the last Godfather. After me, after I join Dante in the empyrean, my family of thirty million or so will not need crime to get on, because in their dark souls and untrustful minds I have placed love and beauty and imagination and understanding. Their olive faces will be raised to the Crystalline Heaven. They will be at the point of assimilation into the American race, prepared to ponder the American Revolution and George Washington and Thomas Jefferson and Alexander Hamilton. They will look into one another's eyes and, instead of sensing alarm, will see brother and sister in Faith, Hope and Charity. (Valerio, *Conversation* 108)

Don Pippo's vision, it turns out, is a life beyond the Italian American enclave, which Nicholas has attempted to lead. It is a life, however, still connected to the Italian American circuit, now a circuit of brother and sisterhood, "Faith, Hope, and Charity", open to all; not a limited, limiting circuit of shame by olive skin or a sense of difference. Don Pippo's vision includes a degree of assimilation as well as allowance for ethnicity, for "Yang the Japanese shoemaker and Bella the female butcher and Juan the Spanish fish vendor and Jake the Jewish pizza maker...Samir, the gay Palestinaian restaurateur, and Gari, the albino Russian musician" (110–11) joined in society with Nicholas the Italian writer.

Valerio's body of work connects Italian American male identity not only to the actions and images of seducers, brutes, and criminals, but also to great Italians and Italian Americans, to the interaction of Italian American men with other Americans, to people of other races and ethnic heritages, and particularly to women. As the final passage of *Lefty* intimates, women—like Odysseus's Penelope, like Dante's Beatrice, like Bandini's Camilla—for men, often symbolize fulfillment. In this passage, Nicholas, speaking to a gathering of the Dante Society of Westchester—at which he meets Lefty, his Beatrice (Hack 4))— tells the story of "the first Italian patriot, Silvio Pellico" (145). Imprisoned in a Venetian dungeon, Pellico, upon seeing women prisoners in a courtyard, exclaims, "'Woman is for me a creature so admirable, so sublime, the mere seeing, hearing and speaking to her enriches my mind with such...'" (146). The ellipses imply Valerio's ambivalence toward Pellico's vision of women. His male characters may expect fulfillment in them, but should they? And will they find it?

In response to this question, Ed Hack, another of the few serious commentators on Valerio's fiction, links *Lefty* to Plato's *Symposium,* to *Magna Graecia,* a cradle of Southern Italian culture. Nicholas believes that he will be made whole in the synergy of his union with Lefty, as Aristophanes believes that the mutual desire for male/female union is really the desire "to recapture the wholeness of personality that existed before Zeus divided us" (Hack 2). Nicholas envies Johnny. "Wherever you go," he tells the don, "your wife and mother make you whole" (Valerio, *Conversation* 71). Later, he declares, "I want to go home, Johnny. That is, I want to make a home with the woman I love. My home doesn't have to be in Brooklyn or Queens or on Staten Island. It could be anywhere on the face of the earth, and I'll buy nice things and learn to care for them. Cook and in my garden grow broccoli–rappe"—which earlier in the novel is a symbol of Nicholas's romantic fulfillment—"and arugula. Despite my age"—around fifty—I'm even thinking of having children. Tell me what to do" (30). Johnny answers with a job offer, which is not, however, a viable solution to Nicholas's romantic dilemma. Nicholas acknowledges to Johnny that the job, as maître d'of a Brooklyn restaurant, would lead him to romance "the widows" (30), women too old and sad to satisfy him. The rest of the novel's romantic plot, Lefty's departure from his life, implies further that Nicholas may have to depend on the memory of interaction with women—and not on women themselves—to make himself whole.

For Valerio's Italian American men, fulfillment means an Italian American identity free of conflicts between Italian custom and American aspiration. Their desire for women to help create that identity may stem from Plato as well as from their intense attachment to Italian culture personified by *La Madonna Santa* and their mothers (Hack 5). Or it simply may echo Dante and Fante in presenting us with the continually disappointed male hope that women will solve the conflicts of time, of space, of society, of ethnicity, by simply loving men.

Valerio presents us, finally, with men who define themselves in relation to women, and who define themselves on the page. His male characters mediate between Italian American subject and American audience, converting Italian American energy into American voltage. Of his first encounter with Johnny, Nicholas recounts, "Our first shared look is hard, wildly physical, at the level of the *coglioni* [testicles]—this is how Italian men know they are men. Light from our hearts shines up to our eyes when we are with our mothers and our children, and sometimes, after giving them a hard time, our women" (*Conversation* 14–15). Tellingly, Nicholas refers to "Italian" and not "Italian American" men in this passage. By emphasizing Italianness, he emphasizes ethnic difference. Yet the mock melodramatic tone of the passage suggests that biology does not, in fact, make the difference; cultural memory does. He and Johnny are certainly American, but they are also, because of their invisible, shared cultural memory, deeply Italian American. Their actions, therefore, require explanation to an American audience.

We should read Valerio's work, then, as an act of ethnic clarification and a symbolic act of resistance to new versions of One Hundred Percent Americanism and to any version of One Hundred Percent Italianism. In addition to (not instead of) a chicken in every pot, a white picket fence, Elvis on every cd player, *Profiles in Courage* in every library, he suggests the possibility of an Italian America: "[T]wo pans of lasagna on every table and a Chrysler mini-van"—the brainchild of Lee Iacocca—"in every garage; Caruso singing in all the parks and from loudspeakers attached to buses and trains; GPO manuals on all the great Italians" (Valerio, *Valentino* 230)—manuals like *Valentino and the Great Italians* itself.

Valentino and Valerio's other books are finally, according to the author, an attempt to "fill a gap in [Italian American] culture" (Valerio, Interview, "Italian"). They fill this gap by connecting contemporary Italian American identities to a rich legacy of positive (as well as negative) history, culture, and myth. They respond to the needs of those Italian Americans who have pursued American economic success and total identification with Anglo American culture, a culture that, in turn, has often taken issue with their ethnicity and neglected the contributions of their Italian American ancestors and contemporaries. They provide electricity for the reanimation of ethnic consciousness (Vecoli, "The Search" 52) in people like Mario Cuomo, whom the narrator, Anthony, addresses directly in *Valentino*.

> Maybe you looked back over your shoulder and didn't see another great Italian politician to style yourself after. After all, there had never been an Italian governor of New York, and you didn't feel quite comfortable styling yourself after a Rockefeller or a Lehman. You say yourself that you inherited very little of Roman sculpture and law and opera and philosophy. That's what I'm here for! Leave it to me to tell you about the Medicis, Machiavelli, Caruso, Petrarca, Benedetto Croce. I fully understand how you feel culturally starved. Sons of immigrants like you and my father and Lee Iacocca and my Uncle Mike—you didn't have the time or motivation to study your culture. You were expected to improve on your parents, uneducated and, as my girlfriend Elsa says, ignorant, to take advantage of the college education they never had by using it to enter the mainstream of American life, blinding you somewhat. But isn't it wonderful, Mr. President, how God created us Italians in such a way that we complement one another so perfectly?" (235).

Here, Valerio raises the possibility—by now a fantasy, as it regards Mario Cuomo—of a bi-culturally connected Italian American President.

Valerio's work provides those who draw their identities from the circuit of Italian American culture (including non–Italian Americans), with a recognizable, usable Italian American past and present. Through a circuitous *ripresa* of Italian and Italian American culture; through reconnection and renegotiation with these cultures via a pastoral Italian American homeland, Valerio's *Valentino and The Great Italians* and *Lefty and the Button Men* take up the *impresa* of rewiring Italian American male identities for viability and new forms of visibility in America.[7]

NOTES

Chapter 1: The Culture that Time Forgot

1. Frederick Douglass favorably compared the living conditions of African American slaves to those of nineteenth-century Southern Italian peasants.

2. Robert Viscusi, in "Narrative and Nothing," illuminates the peasants' experience of nothingness, its role in understanding the society Verga portrays, and its impact on immigrant and later Italian American authors.

> The *cafoni* [peasants], unlike the authorities, do not need to be divided among themselves in order to be rendered harmless. Their separation is of a different kind. They're removed from the drama of power by three layers of Nothing. And even these are precise. At the top, under the guards and dogs, there is that Nothing closest to the rich and powerful. Let us call this **The Nothing of the Deaf**: in *Fontamara*, the rich systematically misinterpret what the *cafoni* say, insisting that every request for help is an act of transgression, and the treating a desperate plea for water as if it were an act of revolutionary terrorism. At the bottom, just above the *cafoni*, there is the Nothing of those who cannot represent themselves. Let us call this **The Nothing of the Mute**: the *cafoni* do not know what to say even when they say it. They arrive at the festival carrying the wrong flag, their clothes are laughable, their accent is sidesplittingly awkward. After all, they *cannot*, actually cannot, speak the language of the nation, but only the local tongue belonging to their narrow little crevasse in the primeval hills—what is called a dialect but has in practice the effect of a visible stigma. They speak with a wordlist and a *cantilena* that mark them out as simply not worth listening to, mark them out no less vividly than a bright red tattoo across the mouth.
>
> Then there is the middle Nothing. It stands for that which cannot even attempt to speak or to hear. This is **The Nothing of the Dead**: it represents that which ought to be there but is not. It represents those who have so totally failed to claim a right to existence that they have either died or emigrated, or both...." (81)

Chapter 2: Americans in the (Un)Making

1. The opening sentence of Harold Toliver's *Pastoral Forms and Attitudes* should help clarify what I mean by "pastoralizing." In it, Toliver addresses

> the broadest implications of the idyllic element of pastoral—usually imaged as a paradisical place where *"Sei piace, ei lice,"* or where "if you like it you may have it" which habitually calls forth an opposite and promotes a variety of "perspective by incongruity." Whether the scene is an explicit Arcadian society or some place of enclosed quiet,

> it or its inhabitants is likely to be exposed to such things as industrialism, death, unrequited love, unjust property division, or merely an opposing idea of perfection. (1)

As in Verga's stories, as in the real lives of Italian immigrants, and as in the constructed lives of immigrant autobiographers.

2. Both James Olney and John Paul Eakin argue that metaphor is "the dominant trope of autobiography" (Eakin 187). In Olney's words,

> The self expresses itself by the metaphors it creates and projects, and we know it by those metaphors; but it did not exist as it now does and as it now is before creating its metaphors. We do not see or touch the self, but we do see and touch its metaphors: and thus we "know" the self, activity or agent, represented in the metaphor and the metaphorizing. (qtd. in Eakin 188)

I take their definition of "metaphor" to mean, broadly, the manifestation of a narrator's use of the fundamental elements of narrative—point of view, plot, character, symbol, setting, diction, theme.

Chapter 3: Family, Beautiful Women and "Stupid Ideas about Writing"

1. The nine books of fiction published to date are the novels *Wait Until Spring, Bandini* (1938), *Ask the Dust* (1939), *Full of Life* (1952), *The Brotherhood of the Grape* (1977), *Dreams from Bunker Hill* (1982), *1933 Was a Bad Year* (1985), and *The Road to Los Angeles* (1985); and the collections *Dago Red* (1940), *The Wine of Youth* (1985), and *West of Rome* (1986).

2. Livorni writes, "another kind of daydreaming will lead Arturo towards the rescue of his ethnic identity: it is the imagined love story with Rosa that leads the young protagonist to recognize himself as Italian" (65).

3. Early stories such as "Big Leaguer" and "The Odyssey of a Wop", and passages of *Wait Until Spring, Bandini*, especially those involving the widow Effie Hildegarde, depict the older Americans' anti-Italian and nativistic behavior.

4. Collins writes, "Baseball has been used *ad nauseum* as a symbol for the American dream, especially in the movies. As a screenwriter himself, Fante was aware of the easy scenarios; and as a writer of serious fiction, he was also aware of the power of the cliché, especially in the way it gives unrealistic hope to certain classes, like the sons of working class immigrants. Fante's contribution to the motif is to show the corrupting power of such boyish dreams, how the moral fabric and the family structure can be undermined in the pursuit of the innocent cliche" (91). To what degree boyhood fantasies can "corrupt" the family, especially Arturo's seemingly impossible prospective family with Rosa, I am not at all certain.

5. It's worth noting that Fante had equal disdain for Italians too devoted to their national system. He wrote his mother in 1935, "Every time I see a picture of those Italian fellows going to war—going like a lot of sheep and yelling 'Duce!' it makes me laugh" (Cooney 107).

6. Silone recreates and explains this conception of life in *Fontamara*. To the peasants of Southern Italy,

> there was the same land, the same rain, the same snow, the same saints' days, the same food, the same anguish, the same pain, and the same misery—the misery received from the fathers, who had inherited it from the grandfathers, and against which honest hard work has never been good for anything. The cruelest injustices there were so old that they took their places among the natural phenomena like the wind, the rain and the snow. The life of the men, the beasts and the land seemed fixed in an inflexible circle…." (15)

7. Fante was also interested in covering the Filipino American scene. Throughout the 1940s, he worked on a novel—which he never completed—to be entitled, "The Little Brown Brother," in which he would "make the little Filipino a hero" (Cooney 175). Fante claimed, "I understand them. I like them. I see them because I am Latin and their tradition, if any, is Spanish and Latin too" (175). For Fante's musings on this unfinished project, see Cooney, *Selected Letters of John Fante 1932–1981*, 175–216.

8. A number of social historians have since written about these processions, with the best account coming from Robert Orsi in *Madonna of 115th Street.*

9. In the 1952 novel *Full of Life*, Fante mocks his own transformation into a "nouveau-riche pseudo-WASP suburbanite" (Cooney 226).

10. For further discussion of twentieth–century novelists' treatment of this theme, see Richard Lehan, "The Los Angeles Novel and the Idea of the West."

11. As I suggested earlier, Grant's treatises on the distinction between "Nordics" (the most intellectually complete group and the group most culturally familiar to "Native" Americans (not American Indians)), "Alpines" (further down on the intellectual and cultural scale), and "Mediterraneans" (the crudest thinkers and the people most alien to "Native American" (Anglo-American) ways). Southern Italians, to Grant's mind, fell into the last category, and, according to commentators like Edward Ross, lacked the rational ability to care for themselves. For similar assessments from the period, see LaGumina, *WOP!* Published three decades ago, *WOP!* remains the best collection of anti-Italian mythology and propaganda available. For an elaboration of Grant's terms, see *The Conquest of a Continent.*

12. Women often functioned, in the words of Jerre Mangione and Ben Morreale, as "family manager"s. For a fuller account of women's obligation and power to hold the family together, see Mangione and Morreale, *La Storia* and Gambino, *Blood of My Blood.*

13. Late in life, Fante, recalling (tongue in cheek?) the experiences on which he based *Ask the Dust,* remarked, "You see, the theme running through *Ask the Dust* is very subtle, and it might even escape some people because I never hit it head on, and that was the fact that I never screwed this girl" (Pleasants 95).

14. In his letters, Fante himself shows an obsessive interest in making money from his writing (Cooney).

Chapter 4: Electric Blue Italian

1. Among other accomplished authors, Helen Barolini, in *Umbertina* (1978), and Robert Viscusi, in *Astoria* (1995), also link their narrators and characters to other figures and events in Italian American cultural history. Standing before the tomb of Napoleon, Viscusi's narrator thinks,

> I began at last to discover in myself, under the character of irascible and disappointed tourist, the incommensurable energies of a pilgrim, arrived at last at what I had been seeking all along in this city full of imperial attitudes: Italy...[Napoleon] was us, Italian to the exact degree he had escaped being Italian, Italy because he had succeeded in escaping Italy, his great originality nothing other than the completeness of his recapitulation of the whole story, the outsider in Italy become an outsider from Italy become a general and a republican become first consul become emperor become his own successor become an exile become an exaggeration in red stone, he was everyone from Romulus and Servius Tullius down through and including Julius Caesar, Machiavelli, Cesare Borgia, Mussolini, and my grandfather, that much of him was as clear as if the pool of tears around his tomb had been filled with the orchestra of La Scala playing *Aida*, clearer, as we were, out of Italy than he could ever have been inside it. (99–100)

2. Those "enclaves were [and to some extent still are] formed of people who had come from the same region or village, sometimes even the same part of a village that had been home for centuries. They clustered together for comfort, for security from the animosity of those who had come from other countries before them, and for the sociability of being with those who spoke their language, ate their foods, and understood their humor and insecurities" (Mangione and Morreale 130).

Salvatore La Puma's *The Boys of Bensonhurst* (1989) presents a portrait of Bensonhurst during World War II that captures the essence of the Italian enclave. The following passage is a fine example.

> Guido worked for the Sicilian Social Society in the storefront under the BMT elevated line on New Utrecht Avenue. Membership in the club was for men only, mostly grandfathers. They sat around and played poker and pinochle, smoked black cigars, drank black coffee, and talked only in the Sicilian dialect...When the men wouldn't be going

home for dinner on time, because they were playing and winning, or playing and losing, Guido would explain matters to the wives. Guido could stand up for the men, and the men knew he wouldn't flirt with their women." (26)

3. In *Through a Glass Darkly,* Boelhower defines "ethnic semiosis" as "nothing more nor less than the interpretive gaze of the subject whose strategy of seeing is determined by the very ethno–symbolic space of the possible world he inhabits" (86–87). It is then a culturally pragmatic gaze.

4. Valerio links his narrator and characters to other "Great Italians" such as Giuseppe Garibaldi, Cesare Pavese, Enrico Caruso, Joe DiMaggio, and Mario Cuomo, by the same means of free association, a discursive movement unfettered by syntactic connection, a habit Valerio calls "part of my nervous system" (Valerio, Interview, "Italian").

5. For more on recent Mafia comedy, see my own piece, published in different versions as "'Cunnilingus and Psychotherapy Brought Us to This': Mafia Comedy as Italian American Cultural Expression," in *The Columbia Journal of American Studies* 5.1 (2002): 82–96, and "Analyze This *Goombah*: Mafia Comedy as Italian American Cultural Expression," in *Italian Americans: A Retrospective on the Twentieth Century.* Chicago Heights: American Italian Historical Association, 2001. 225–244. See also two recent collections of critical articles, *A Sitdown with the Sopranos.* Ed. Regina Barreca. New York: Palgrave, 2002, and *This Thing of Ours: Investigating the Sopranos.* Ed. David Lavery. New York: Columbia UP, 2002.

6. Valerio admits in his interview with Leonard Lopate, "I felt, as I was creating [*Lefty and the Button Men*], that I have the potential for both [don and sensitive lover/artist], as I think maybe many Italian Americans would feel."

7. Valerio's current project—a memoir of his life with the Toni Cade Bambara and his relationships with other African American writers and cultural workers—promises the exploration of other American identities as well.

Bibliography

Aesop. *Aesop's Fables*. New York: Lancer Books, 1968.

Addams, Jane. *Twenty Years at Hull House.* 1910. New York: Signet Classics, 1981.

Alba, Richard D. *Italian Americans: Into the Twilight of Ethnicity.* Englewood Cliffs, NJ: Prentice–Hall Inc., 1985.

Alger, Horatio, Jr. *Phil, the Fiddler or, The Story of a Young Street Musician.* 1872. North Plainfield, N. J., 1971.

Anzaldúa, Gloria. *Borderlands/La Frontera: The New Meztiza.* San Francisco: Spinsters/Aunt Lute, 1987.

Analyze This. Dir. Ivan Reitman. Perf. Robert DeNiro, Billy Crystal. Warner Brothers, 1999.

Archdeacon, Thomas J. *Becoming American: An Ethnic History.* New York: The Free Press, 1983.

Barolini, Helen, ed. *The Dream Book: An Anthology of Writings of Italian American Women.* New York: Schoken Books, 1985.

———. *Umbertina.* Salem, N. H.: Ayer Publishers, 1979.

Barreca, Regina, ed. *A Sitdown with the Sopranos: Watching Italian American Culture on T.V.'s Most Talked–About Series.* New York: Palgrave, 2002.

Barzini, Luigi. *The Italians: A Full–Length Portrait Featuring Their Manners and Morals.* New York: Atheneum, 1964.

Bhabha, Homi K. *Nation and Narration.* New York: Routledge, 1990.

Boelhower, William. "The Brave New World of Immigrant." *MELUS* 9.2 (1982): 5–23.

———. *Immigrant Autobiography in the United States.* Verona: Essedue Edizioni, 1982.

———. *Through a Glass Darkly: Ethnic Semiosis in American Literature.* New York: Oxford UP, 1987.

Bona, Mary Jo, ed. *The Voices We Carry: Recent Italian/American Women's Fiction.* Toronto: Guernica Editions, 1994.

Cahan, Abraham. *The Rise of David Levinsky.* 1917. New York: Harper Torchbooks, 1960.

Calvino, Italo. *Italian Folktales.* 1956. Trans. George Martin. New York: Pantheon Books, 1981.

Cannistraro, Philip V. *Blackshirts in Little Italy: Italian Americans and Fas-*

cism 1921–1929. West Lafayette, IN: Bordighera Press, 1999.
Capellini, Giovanni. *Ricordi di un viaggio scientifico nell' America settentrionale nel MDCCCLXIII.* Bologna: Giseppe Vitali, 1867.
Carnevali, Emanuel. *The Autobiography of Emanuel Carnevali.* Ed. Kay Boyle. New York: Horizon Press, 1967.
Carravetta, Peter, ed. *Differentia.* 6–7 (Summer/Autumn 1994).
Carravetta, Peter. "Valentino and the Great Italians." in Carravetta 347–355.
Cawelti, John G. *Apostles of the Self–Made Man.* Chicago: U of Chicago P, 1965.
Cecchetti, Giovanni. *Giovanni Verga.* Boston: Twayne Publishers, 1978.
———. Introduction. *The She–Wolf and Other Stories.* Trans. Giovanni Cecchetti. By Giovanni Verga. Berkeley: U of California P, 1973. v–xx.
Ciongoli, A Kenneth and Jay Parini, eds. *Beyond the Godfather: Italian American Writers on the Real Italian American Experience.* Hanover, N. H.: U of New England P, 1997.
Cipolla, Gaetano. "Thomas Augustine Daly: An Early Voice of the Italian Immigrants." *Italian Americana* 6.1 (1980): 45–59.
Collins, Richard. "Fante's Families and the Epiphany of Failure." in Cooper and Fine. 95–111.
———. "Of Wops, Dagoes, and Filipinos: John Fante and the Immigrant Experience." *The Redneck Review of Literature* 21 (1991): 44–48.
———. "Stealing Home: John Fante and the Moral Dimension of Baseball." *Aethlon* 12.1 (1994): 81–91.
Cooney, Seamus, ed. *John Fante: Selected Letters 1932–1980.* Santa Rosa: Black Sparrow Press, 1991.
Cooper, J. C. *An Illustrated Encyclopaedia of Traditional Symbols.* London: Thames and Hudson, 1978.
Cooper, Stephen. "John Fante's Eternal City." in Fine. 83–99.
———. *Full of Life: A Biography of John Fante.* New York: North Point Press, 2000.
Cooper, Stephen and David Fine, eds. *John Fante: A Critical Gathering.* Madison, NJ: Fairleigh Dickinson UP, 1999.
Corresca, Rocco. "The Biography of a Bootblack." 1902. *PlainFolk: The Life Stories of Undistinguished Americans.* Ed. David M. Katzman and William M. Tuttle, Jr. Urbana:U of Illinois P, 1982.
Covello, Leonard. *The Social Background of the Italo–American School-Child.* Leiden: E. J. Brill, 1967.

Curran, Thomas. *Xenophobia and Immigration, 1820–1930.* Boston: Twayne Publishers, 1975.

Daly, Thomas Augustine. *McAroni Ballads.* New York: Harcourt, Brace and Howe, 1919.

D'Angelo, Pascal. *Son of Italy.* New York: MacMillan, 1924.

Decker, Jeffrey Louis. *Made in America: Self–Styled Success from Horatio Alger to Oprah Winfrey.* Minneapolis: U of Minnesota P, 1997.

DeConde, Alexander. "Endearment or Antipathy?: Nineteenth Century American Attitudes toward Italians." *Ethnic Groups* 4 (1982): 131–48.

Dégh, Linda. "Folk Narrative." *Folklore and Folklife: An Introduction.* Ed. Richard M. Dorson. Chicago: U of Chicago P, 1972. 53–83.

De Marco Torgovnik, Marianna. *Crossing Ocean Parkway.* Chicago: U of Chicago P, 1994.

De Rosa, Gabriele. *Chiesa e religione popolare nel Mezzogiorno.* Roma-Bari: Laterza, 1978.

Do the Right Thing. Dir. Spike Lee. Universal, 1989.

Dos Passos, John. *U.S.A.* Illus. Reginald Marsh. Boston: Houghton Mifflin, 1963.

Douglass, William A. *Emigration in a South Italian Town.* New Brunswick, N. J.: Rutgers UP, 1984.

Eakin, Paul John. *Fictions in Autobiography: Studies in the Art of Self–Invention.* Princeton: Princeton UP, 1985.

Eliot, T. S. *Collected Poems 1909–1962.* New York: Harcourt Brace Jovanovich, 1963.

Equiano, Olaudah. "The Interesting Narrative of the Life of Olaudah Equiano." *The Classic Slave Narratives.* Comp. and ed. Henry Louis Gates, Jr. New York: New American Library, 1987. 1–182.

Fante, John. *Ask the Dust.* 1939. Santa Rosa: Black Sparrow Press, 1980.

———. *The Brotherhood of the Grape.* 1977. Santa Rosa: Black Sparrow Press, 1988.

———. *Dago Red.* New York: Viking Press, 1940.

———. *Dreams from Bunker Hill.* Santa Rosa: Black Sparrow Press, 1982.

———. *Full of Life.* 1952. Santa Rosa: Black Sparrow Press, 1987.

———. *1933 Was a Bad Year.* Santa Rosa: Black Sparrow Press, 1985.

———. *The Road to Los Angeles.* Santa Rosa: Black Sparrow Press, 1985.

———. *Wait Until Spring, Bandini.* 1938. Santa Rosa: Black Sparrow Press, 1983.

———. *West of Rome.* Santa Rosa: Black Sparrow Press, 1986.

———. *The Wine of Youth.* Santa Rosa: Black Sparrow Press, 1991.

Fine, David, ed. *Los Angeles in Fiction: A Collection of Essays.* Albuquerque: U of New Mexico P, 1995.

Fink, Rychard. "Introduction." in Alger.

Ferlinghetti, Lawrence. "The Old Italians Dying." in Gillan and Gillan. 15–17.

Fitzgerald, F. Scott. *The Great Gatsby.* 1925. New York: Collier Books,1980.

Fontana, Ferdinando. *Viaggi.* Milano: F. Fontana Editore, 1893.

The Four Horsemen. Dir. Rex Ingram. Perf. Rudolph Valentino. Metro Pictures, 1921.

Franklin, Benjamin. *The Autobiography.* 1868. *The Norton Anthology of American Literature, Vol. I.* 3rd Edition. Ed. Francis Murphy. New York: W. W. Norton and Co., 1989.

Gabaccia, Donna R. *From Sicily to Elizabeth Street: Housing and Social Change among Italian Immigrants, 1880–1930.* Albany: SUNY P, 1984.

Gambino, Richard. *Blood of My Blood.* New York: Anchor Books, 1975.

———."The Crisis of Italian American Identity." in Ciongoli and Parini. 269–288.

Gardaphé, Fred. *Dagoes Read.* Toronto: Guernica, 1996.

———."From Oral Tradition to Written Work: Toward an Ethnographically Based Literary Criticism." in Tamburri, Giordano and Gardaphé. 294–306.

———. "In Search of Italian/American Writers." *Italian America.* March 1997: 6–10.

———. *Italian Signs, American Streets: The Evolution of Italian American Narrative.* Durham: Duke UP, 1996.

Gardini, Carlo. *Gli Stati Uniti ricordi con 76 illustrazioni e carte.* 2nd ed. Bologna: Nicola Zanichelli, 1891.

Gardner, Ralph D. *Horatio Alger or the American Hero Era.* 1964. New York: Arco Publishing, 1978.

Gillan, Maria Mazziotti. "Growing Up Italian." in Gillan and Gillan. 382–84.

Gillan, Maria Mazziotti and Jennifer Gillan, eds. *Unsettling America.* New York: Penguin, 1994.

Giunta, Edvige. "Italian/American Women Authors." *Voices in Italian Americana* 7.2 (1996): i–iii.

———. *Writing with an Accent: Contemporary Italian American Women Authors*. New York: Palgrave, 2002.

Glazer, Nathan and Daniel Patrick Moynihan. *Beyond the Melting Pot*. Cambridge, Mass.: The M. I. T. P, 1963.

The Godfather. Dir. Francis Ford Coppola. Paramount, 1972.

The Godfather Part II. Dir. Francis Ford Coppola. Paramount, 1974.

Goodfellas. Dir. Martin Scorsese. Warner Brothers, 1990.

Gramsci, Antonio. *Selections from the Prison Notebooks*. Ed. and Trans. Quentin Hoare and Geoffrey Nowell Smith. NewYork: International Publishers, 1971.

Grant, Madison. *The Conquest of a Continent*. New York: Charles Scribner's Sons, 1933.

———. *The Passing of the Great Race or The Racial Basis of European History*. New York: Charles Scribner's Sons, 1916.

Green, Rose Basile. *The Italian–American Novel: A Document of the Interaction of Two Cultures*. Rutherford: Fairleigh Dickinson UP, 1974.

Guida, George. "Analyze This *Goombah*: Mafia Comedy as Italian American Cultural Expression." in Sensi–Isolani and Tamburri. 225–244.

———. "'Cunnilingus and Psychotherapy Brought Us to This': Mafia Comedy as Italian American Cultural Expression." *The Columbia Journal of American Studies* 5.1 (2002): 82–96.

———. "In Imagination of the Past: Fante's *Ask the Dust* as Italian American Modernism." in Cooper and Fine. 131–144.

———. "Novel Paesans: The Reconstruction of Italian American Male Identity in Anthony Valerio's *Conversation with Johnny* and Robert Viscusi's *Astoria*." *MELUS* 26.2 (Summer 2001): 95–109.

Hack, Edward. Unpublished essay, 1998.

Haley, Alex. *Roots*. New York: Doubleday, 1976.

Haller, Hermann W. *Una lingua perduta e ritrovata*. Scandicci (Firenze): La Nuova Italia Editrice, 1993.

Handlin, Oscar. *The Uprooted*. 2nd ed. Boston: Atlantic Monthly Press, 1973.

Hemingway, Ernest. *The Sun Also Rises*. New York: Charles Scribner's Sons, 1926.

Higham, John. *Strangers in the Land: Patterns of American Nativism 1860–1925*. New Brunswick: Rutgers UP, 1955.

Hijuelos, Oscar. *The Mambo Kings Play Songs of Love*. 1989. Harper and Row, 1990.

Holman, C. Hugh. "Hemingway and Vanity Fair." in Wagner. 139–146.
Holte, James Craig. "Benjamin Franklin and Italian–American Narratives." *MELUS* 5.4 (1978): 99–102.
———. "The Newcomer in America: A Study of Italian and Puerto Rican–American Personal Narratives." Diss. U of Cincinnati, 1978.
———. "Private Lives and Public Faces: Ethnic American Autobiography." *Ethnic Groups* 4.1–2 (1982): 61–83.
———. "The Representative Voice: Autobiography and the Ethnic Experience." *MELUS* 9.2 (1982): 25–46.
Iorizzo, Luciano T. and Salvatore Mondello. *The Italian Americans.* Revised Ed. Boston: Twayne Publishers, 1980.
Jacobs, Harriet. "Incidents in the Life of a Slave Girl." *The Classic Slave-Narratives.* Comp. and ed. Henry Louis Gates, Jr. New York: New American Library, 1987. 243–332.
Jeanne Eagels. Screenplay by John Fante. Columbia, 1957.
Jones, Maldwyn Allen. *American Immigration.* 2nd ed. Chicago: U of Chicago P, 1992.
Johnson, Charles. *Middle Passage.* New York: Atheneum, 1990.
Jungle Fever. Dir. Spike Lee. Universal, 1991.
Kennedy, John F. and Robert F. Kennedy. *Profiles in Courage.* 1956. New York: HarperCollins, 1989.
LaGumina, Salvatore, ed. *WOP!: A Documentary History of Anti–Italian Discrimination in the United States.* San Francisco: Straight Arrow Books, 1973.
La Puma, Salvatore. *The Boys of Bensonhurst.* Athens, GA: U of Georgia P, 1987.
La Sorte, Michael. *La Merica: Images of Italian Greenhorn Experience.* Philadelphia: Temple UP, 1985.
The Last Don. Dir. Graeme Clifford. Trimark, 1997.
The Last Don II. Dir. Graeme Clifford. Konigsberg–Sonitzky, 1998.
Lavery, David, ed. *This Thing of Ours: Investigating the Sopranos.* New York: Columbia UP, 2002.
Lehan, Richard. "The Los Angeles Novel and the Idea of the West," in Fine. 29–41.
Lejeune, Philippe. *On Autobiography.* Trans. Katherine Leary. Ed. J. P. Eakin. Minneapolis: U of Minnesota P, 1989.
Litz, Walton A, ed. *American Writers: A Collection of Literary Biographies.*

Supplement II, Part I. Detroit: Gale Research Co., 1978.

Livorni, Ernesto. "John Fante: 'The Saga of Arturo Bandini'." *Voices in Italian Americana* 6.1 (1995): 52–73.

Lucente, Gregory L. "The Ideology of Form in Verga's 'La Lupa': Realism, Myth, and the Passion of Control." *MLN* 95.1 (1980): 104–38.

McManus, Walter S. "Labor Market Assimilation of Immigrants: The Importance of Language Skills." *Contemporary Policy Issues* 3.3 (1985): 77–89.

Mack Smith, Denis. *Italy: A Modern History*. Ann Arbor: U of Michigan P, 1959.

Mangione, Jerre and Ben Morreale. *La Storia: Five Centuries of the Italian American Experience*. New York: HarperCollins, 1992.

Manoukian, Agopik. "La Famiglia dei contadini." *La Famiglia italiana dall'Ottocento a oggi*. Ed. Piero Melograni, with Lucetta Scaraffia. Roma–Bari: Laterza, 1988. 3–60.

Marinelli, Peter. *Pastoral*. The Critical Idiom Series. 15. London: Methuen and Co., 1971.

Martin, Jay. "John Fante: The Burden of Modernism." in Cooper and Fine. 17–41.

Martin, Mick and Marsha Porter. *Video Movie Guide 1997*. New York: Ballantine Books, 1996.

Maso, Carole. *Ghost Dance*. Hopewell, NJ: The Ecco Press, 1986.

Massa, Ann, ed. *American Declarations of Love*. New York: Brooklyn College Press, 1990.

Miele, Stefano. Autobiographical Sketch. in Iorizzo, and Mondello 150–152.

Moore, Jack B. "Understanding Joe DiMaggio as an American Hero." in De Sena, Judith N. and Jerome Krase. *Italian Americans in a Multicultural Society*. Stony Brook: Forum Italicum, 1994. 169–78.

Morrison, Toni. *Beloved*. 1987. New York: Signet, 1991.

Nelli, Humbert. *From Immigrants to Ethnics: The Italian Americans*. New York: Oxford UP, 1983.

Nietzsche, Friedrich. *Beyond Good and Evil*. 1886. Trans. R. J. Hollingdale. New York: Penguin, 1990.

Il Nuovo Zingarelli minore: vocabolario della lingua Italiana di Nicola Zingarelli. 11th ed. Bologna: Zanichelli, 1987.

O'Grady, Deirdre. "The Vicious Circle: Giovanni Verga as Storyteller." *Italian Storytellers: Essays on Italian Narrative Literature*. Eds. Eric

Haywood and Cormac Ó Cuilleanáin. Dublin: Irish Academic P, 1989. 204–228.

O. Henry (William Sidney Porter). *The Four Million.* New York: Doubleday, Page & Company, 1906.

Olney, James, ed. *Studies in Autobiography.* New York: Oxford UP, 1988.

Ornitz, Samuel. *Haunch, Paunch, and Jowl: An Anonymous Autobiography.* New York: Boni and Liveright, 1923.

Orsi, Robert. "The Fault of Memory: 'Southern Italy' in the Imagination of Immigrants and the Lives of Their Children in Italian Harlem, 1920–1945." *The Journal of Family History* 15.2 (1990): 133–47.

———. *The Madonna of 115th Street: Faith and Community in Italian Harlem, 1880–1950.* New Haven: Yale UP, 1988.

———. "The Religious Boundaries of an Inbetween People: Street *Feste* and the Problem of the Dark–Skinned Other in Italian Harlem, 1920–1990." *American Quarterly* 44.3 (1992): 313–47.

Pacifici, Sergio. "The Tragic World of Verga's Primitives." *From Verismo to Experimentalism: Essays on the Modern Italian Novel.* Ed. Sergio Pacifici. Bloomington: Indiana UP, 1969. 4–38.

Panunzio, Constantine. *Immigration Crossroads.* New York: MacMillan, 1927.

———. *The Soul of an Immigrant.* New York: MacMillan, 1921.

Parrino, Maria, ed. *Italian American Autobiographies.* Intr. Richard Gambino. Providence: Italian Americana Publications, 1993.

Pasolini, Pier Paolo, ed. *Canzoniere italiano: Antologia della poesia popolare.* Vol 2. Milan: Garzanti Editore, 1992.

Patti, Samuel J. "Autobiography: The Root of Italian American Narrative." *Annali d'Italianistica* 4 (1986): 243–48.

———. "Recent Italian American Literature: The Case of John Fante." in Tamburri, Giordano, and Gardaphé. 329–337.

Pei, Mario. Preface. *The Golden Carnation and Other Stories Told in Italy.* Frances Toor. New York: Lothrop, Lee and Shepard Co., 1960. vii–x.

Phipard, Charles B. "The Philanthropist–Padrone." *Charities* 12 (1904): 470–72.

Pleasants, Ben. "The Last Interview of John Fante." *Los Angeles* 39 (1994): 90–95.

Propp, Vladimir. *Theory and History of Folklore.* Trans. Adriadna Y. Martin and Richard P. Martin and several others. Ed. Anatoly Lieberman. Minneapolis: U of Minneapolis P, 1984.

Puzo, Mario. *The Godfather*. New York: G. P. Putnam's Sons, 1969.

Rando, Flavia. "'My Mother Was a Strong Woman': Respect, Shame, and the Feminine Body in the Sculpture of Nancy Azara and Antonette Rosato." *Voices in Italian Americana* 7.2 (1996): 21–34.

Reluctant Saint. Screenplay by John Fante. Dir. Edward Dmytryk. Dmytryk Weiler, 1962.

Reynolds, Michael S. The Sun Also Rises: *A Student's Companion to the Novel*. Boston: Twayne Publishers, 1988.

Riis, Jacob. *The Making of an American.* 1901. New York: The MacMillan Company, 1937.

Rolle, Andrew. *The Italian Americans: Troubled Roots.* New York: The Free Press, 1980.

Romano, Rose. "But My Blood." in Gillan and Gillan. 194–95.

Ross, Edward Alsworth. *The Old World in the New: The Significance of Past and Present Immigration to the American People.* New York: The Century Co., 1914.

Russo, John Paul. "From Italophilia to Italophobia: Representations of Italian Americans in the Gilded Age." in Carravetta. 45–75.

Russo, Pietro. "The Italian American Periodical Press, 1836–1980." *Italian Americans: New Perspectives in Italian Immigration and Ethnicity*. Ed. Lydio F. Tomasi. New York: Center or Migration Studies, 1985. 248–59.

Salomone–Marino, Salvatore. *Customs and Habits of the Sicilian Peasant.* 1897. Trans. and Ed. Rosalie N. Norris, from *Costumi e usanze di contadini di Sicilia*. Ed. Aurelio Rigoli. 1968. Rutherford, NJ: Fairleigh Dickinson UP, 1981.

Saturday Night Fever. Dir. John Badham. Paramount, 1977.

Saturday Night Live. Various Episodes. National Broadcasting Company. WNBC.

Savana, A. V. and M. L. Straniero, eds. *Canti dell'emigrazione*. Milan: Garzanti Editore, 1976.

Scapp, Ron. "Watermelons, Tee Shirts and Giorgio Armani: Eight–and–a–Half Epigrams on Italian–American Culture." in Carravetta. 33–44.

Schwab, Gariele. "Reader–Response and the Aesthetic Experience of Otherness." *The Stanford Literature Review* 3.1 (1986): 107–36.

Selig, Karl–Ludwig. "Reading Verga's 'Rosso Malpelo'." *Teaching Lan-*

guage Through Literature 26.2 (1987): 33–39.

Silone, Ignazio. *Fontamara.* 1934. Revised ed. Trans. Harvey Fergusson II. New York: Dell Publishing, 1960.

Simon, Rita J. *Public Opinion and the Immigrant: Print Media Coverage, 1880–1980.* Lexington, MA: Lexington Books, 1985.

Sollors, Werner. *Beyond Ethnicity.* New York: Oxford UP, 1986.

The Sopranos. Creat. David Chase. Perf. James Gandolfini, Nancy Marchand, Lorraine Bracco, Edie Falco. Various episodes. Home Box Office. 1999–2001.

Sori, Ercole. *L'Emigrazione italiana dall'Unità alla Seconda Guerra Mondiale.* Bologna: Il Mulino, 1979.

Spengemann, William C. and L. R. Lundquist. "Autobiography and the American Myth." *American Quarterly* 17.3 (1965): 501–519.

Spotnitz, Frank. "The Hottest Dead Man in Hollywood." *American Film* 14 (July/Aug 1989): 40+.

Spagnoletti, Giacinto and Cesare Vivaldi, eds. *Poesia dialettale dal Rinascimento a oggi, volume secondo.* Milan: Garzanti, 1991.

Stead, Alistair. "Pastoral Sexuality in British and American Fiction." *Forked Tongues?: Comparing Twentieth–Century British and American Literature.* Eds. Ann Massa and Alistair Stead. London: Longman, 1994.

Steele, Richard W. "The War on Intolerance: The Reformulation of American Nationalism, 1939–1941." *American Ethnic History* 9.1 (1989): 9–35.

Summer of Sam. Dir. Spike Lee. Universal, 1999.

Symonds, John Addington. *Renaissance in Italy: Italian Literature, Part I.* 1881. New York: Capricorn Books, 1964.

Takaki, Ronald. *A Different Mirror: A History of Multicultural America.* Boston: Little, Brown & Co., 1993.

Tamburri, Anthony Julian. "In (Re)cognition of the Italian/American Writer: Definitions and Categories." in Carravetta 9–32.

Tamburri, Anthony J. and Paolo A. Giordano, eds. *Beyond the Margin: Readings in Italian Americana.* Teaneck, N. J.: Fairleigh Dickinson UP, 1998.

Tamburri, Anthony Julian, Paolo A. Giordano and Fred L. Gardaphé, eds. *From the Margin: Writings in Italian Americana.* West Lafayette: Purdue UP, 1991.

Tomasi di Lampedusa, Giuseppe. *The Leopard [Il Gattopardo].* 1958. Trans.

Archibald Colquhoun. New York: Signet, 1960.

Toliver, Harold. *Pastoral Forms and Attitudes.* Berkeley: U of California P, 1971.

Toschi, Paolo. *Invito al folklore italiano: Le Regioni e le feste.* Roma: Editrice Stadium, 1963.

Valerio, Anthony. *Anita Garibaldi.* Westport, CT: Praeger, 2001.

———. *Bart: A Life of A Bartlett Giamatti by Him and About Him.* New York: Harcourt Brace Jovanovich, 1991.

———. "BlackItalian." Unpublished memoir, 2003.

———. *Conversation with Johnny.* Toronto: Guernica Editions, 1997.

———. Interview with George Guida. *Italian Matters.* Public Access Television, New York, 7 Feb. 1995.

———. Interview with Leonard Lopate. *New York and Company.* Natl. Public Radio. WNYC, New York. 7 August 1997.

———. *Lefty and the Button Men.* Philadelphia: Xlibris Corporation, 2000.

———. *The Mediterranean Runs through Brooklyn.* New York: H. B. Davis, 1982.

———. Personal interview. 5 December 1996.

———. "The Skyjacker." *The Paris Review.* 73 (Winter 1977): 80–86.

———. *Valentino and The Great Italians.* 1986. Toronto: Guernica Editions, 1994.

———. "Water for Toni Morrison." *Voices in Italian Americana*7.1 (1996): 99–104.

Vecoli, Rudolph J. "The Search for an Italian American Identity." *Rivista di studi anglo–americani* 3 (1984): 29–65.

Ventresca, Francesco. *Personal Reminiscences of a Naturalized American.* New York: Daniel Ryerson, Inc., 1937.

Verdicchio, Pasquale. "Spike Lee's Guineas." in Carravetta. 177–92.

Verga, Giovanni. *Maestro Don Gesualdo.* 1889. New York: Greenwood Press, 1976.

———. *I Malavoglia.* 1881. New York: Schoenhofs Foreign Books, 1991.

———. *Tutte le novelle.* New York: Schoenhofs Foreign Books, 1950.

———. *The She–Wolf [La Lupa] and Other Stories.* Trans. Giovanni Cecchetti. Berkeley: U of California P, 1973.

Viscusi, Robert. *Astoria.* Toronto: Guernica Editions, 1995.

———. "*De Vulgari Eloquentia:* An Approach to the Language of Italian American Fiction." *Yale Italian Studies* 1 (Winter 1981) 21–38.

———. “Debate in the Dark: Love in Italian American Fiction.” in Massa. 155–163.

———. “Narrative and Nothing: The Enterprise of Italian American Writing.” in Carravetta. 77–99.

Wagner, Linda W., ed. *Ernest Hemingway: Six Decades of Criticism.* East Lansing: Michigan State UP, 1987.

Walk on the Wild Side. Screenplay by John Fante. Dir. Edward Dmytryk. Columbia, 1962.

West, Nathanael. *The Day of the Locust.* 1939. New York: New Directions, 1962.

Williams, Raymond. *The Country and the City.* New York: Oxford UP, 1973.

Wills, Ross B. “John Fante.” in Cooney. 329–338.

Woolf, D. *The Art of Verga: A Study in Objectivity.* Sydney: Sydney UP, 1977.

Wyllie, Irvin G. *The Self-Made Man in America: The Myth of Rags to Riches.* New Brunswick, N. J.: Rutgers UP, 1954.

INDEX